LAK CHANG

A reconstruction of Tai identity in Daikong

Yos Santasombat

ANU
THE AUSTRALIAN NATIONAL UNIVERSITY

E PRESS

ANU
E PRESS

Published by ANU E Press
The Australian National University
Canberra ACT 0200, Australia
Email: anuepress@anu.edu.au

Cover: The bride (right) dressed for the first time as a married woman.

Previously published by Pandanus Books

National Library in Australia Cataloguing-in-Publication entry

      Santasombat, Yos.
      Lak Chang : a reconstruction of Tai identity in Daikong.

Author: Yos Santasombat.

Title: Lak chang : a reconstruction of Tai identity in Daikong /
           Yos Santasombat.

ISBN: 9781921536380 (pbk.)

            9781921536397 (pdf)

Notes: Bibliography.

Subjects: Tai (Southeast Asian people)--China--Yunnan Province.

Other Authors/Contributors:

         Thai-Yunnan Project.

Dewey Number: 306.089959105135

LAK CHANG

A reconstruction of Tai identity in Daikong

For my father

CONTENTS

PREFACE

The Thai–Yunnan Project of The Australian National University is proud to present the English-langauge version of Professor Yos Santasombat's fascinating ethnography of the Tai in Daikong, southwestern China. This work, originally published in Thai in 2000,[1] is a significant contribution to the ethnographic record of the Tai peoples and, at the same time, a fascinating insight into the current state of ethnography produced within the Thai–Yunnan region. In the preface to the Thai edition of the work, Chatthip Nartsupha suggests that this is the first ethnography of the Tai outside Thailand conducted by a Thai scholar and, as such, the book is an important example of the intersection between "local" and "academic" imaginings in the construction and reconstruction of ethnic identity in the Tai—and Thai—worlds.[2]

Readers who are familiar with Thai or Lao culture will find much that is reassuring in this account of life in Lak Chang. Here, in the borderlands of Yunnan province, southwestern China, are Tai farmers cultivating rice in irrigated paddy fields; exchanging labour for transplanting and harvesting; referring to their fellow villagers as *pi* and *nong*; and unselfconsciously combining "spirit beliefs" with Theravada Buddhism. The local language is intelligible, though with some difficulty, to a Thai speaker. Little wonder that one important aspect of the recent renewal of cross-border linkages in the Thai–Yunnan region has been a growing interest—often imbued with nostalgia, a little fantasy and the occasional dash of chauvinism—in the spatial and temporal continuities of Tai-ness (and, for some, Thai-ness). These various attempts "to construct the distant past by studying the geographically distant" (page 16) respond nicely to a widely felt desire for cultural continuity in a space and time of economic, social and environmental transformation.

Of course, in the village of Lak Chang the Tai world is increasingly embraced by the Han Chinese world. Professor Yos skilfully weaves ethnographic and historical

1 *Lak Chang: Kan sang mai khong athalak tai nai Daikong*. Bangkok: Project on Tai Culture and Social History, Withithad, 2000.
2 See the author's footnote on page xi for his definition of "Tai" and "Thai".

writing to chart the course of Lak Chang's incorporation into the modern Chinese state. His account of the period of agricultural cooperatives and communes provides important insight into the impact on predominantly household-based farming systems of an ideologically driven over-emphasis on communal arrangements. Similarly his account of the naïve brutality of the Cultural Revolution—culminating in the humiliation and death of the local Tai prince, the chaopha—is a potent case-study of the Chinese state's assault at the time on minority authority structures and value systems. "Our objective", the villagers of Lak Chang were told, "was to struggle against the ideology of the bourgeoisie and all other ruling classes, and to transform education, literature and art and all other parts of the superstructure not in correspondence with the socialist economic base so as to facilitate the consolidation and development of socialism" (page 33).

However, the darkest periods are now in the past and what is striking about this book is its feeling of optimism. Professor Yos proposes a sense of Tai identity that is relatively flexible, adaptive and incorporative. In the course of the study it becomes clear that the boundary between Han and Tai—while clearly demarcated—is characterised by considerable symbolic and material passage. The influence of Han culture on housebuilding, architectural symbolism, weddings, funerals, clothing and consumer spending is clearly evident. Professor Yos is fully aware of the realities of unequal power but he argues, in a crucial passage, that "[p]erhaps, the Tai Yai emulation of Han characteristics is not just distorted imitation, but has become, rather, a constitutive element in Tai Yai's lives" (page 15). While acknowledging the persistent influence of primordialism in Tai studies, Professor Yos makes a strong case for a sense of ethnicity that is, to a considerable extent, a strategic refashioning of historical consciousness in response to contemporary concerns. In this fundamentally political endeavour—from which I doubt Professor Yos excludes himself—there may even be a place for a dose of primordialism given that timelessness itself "may be situationally constructed" (page 13).

A particular feature of the optimism of this ethnography is the relatively benign presence of the market. The level of engagement with the market of Lak Chang's villagers is little short of astounding. What appear to be enormously productive and relatively abundant agricultural lands enable Lak Chang's villagers to sell a large percentage of their agricultural production to Chinese and Tai traders, while still maintaining a secure subsistence base. There is little evidence that this substantial engagement with the market has undermined either village solidarity or a distinctive—yet flexible—sense of local identity. Indeed there are strong indications that agricultural commercialisation, and attendant pressures on land, has strengthened villager determination to maintain local control of the all-important paddy fields, perhaps leading to a strengthening of the preference for village endogamy. Similarly, pressures on dry-season labour resources have led to the *poi* festival each year becoming primarily a village undertaking rather than an opportunity for relatively well-resourced households to enhance their merit and prestige. Lavish spending on wedding feasts provides new avenues for household prestige but, at the same time, certain elements of the wedding ceremony provide opportunities to make culturally distinct statements about Tai-ness.

The research for this work was supported by the Thailand Research Fund as part of the Project on the Social and Cultural History of the Tai Peoples. In the preface to the Thai edition Chatthip expresses the hope that this project will assist in discovering the common roots of Tai cultures and in documenting the various cultural histories of the Tai peoples. Professor Yos has made an important contribution to achieving this goal and, perhaps most importantly, persuasively demonstrates that close engagement with other cultural, political and economic systems, while sometimes extraordinarily painful, need not diminish a distinctive and dynamic sense of local identity.

Andrew Walker
Canberra
April 2001

ACKNOWLEDGEMENTS

I began pursuing the idea of doing fieldwork among the Tai ethnic minority[1] group in Yunnan twenty years ago when I was a graduate student at Berkeley. China later became a tempting destination left off the itinerary in the early 1980s when a graduate student from Stanford published an article in a Taiwanese newspaper on abortion practices in China. After that it became increasingly difficult for students from American institutes to obtain permission to do field research in rural China.

But the prospects remained within me throughout the years and when Professor Chatthip Nartsupha, head of the Tai History and Culture Studies Project, invited me to join him on a trip to Daikong, Yunnan, I readily accepted his invitation. In March 1997, I bid him goodbye in Kunming and took my family to Muang Khon in Daikong prefecture. The task I had set myself—indeed, the general theme which sustains my study—is to discover how, over the last four centuries of Chinese domination, the Tai groups in Daikong managed to maintain a strong sense of cultural continuity and ethnic identity.

After a brief survey of Tai villages in Muang Khon, Muang Wan, Muang La, Muang Ti and Muang Mao, I chose Lak Chang village as my research site for several reasons. First of all, compared to other villages in Daikong, Lak Chang was rather small (203 households) and hence more manageable as a research unit. More importantly, the villagers of Lak Chang impressed me in various ways. Even though most villagers now live in wattle and daub houses with cement floors and

---

1 I use the term Tai to refer to various Tai ethnic groups in Southeast Asia and its periphery, such as the Tai Ahom of Assam in India, the Shan of Shan State in Myanmar, the Tai Daikong in Yunnan, the Tai Lue in Laos, the Tai Dam, Tai Dang and Tai Khao in Sipsong Chu Tai and Vietnam, including the Zhuang and the Dong of Kweichou, Hunan and Kwangsi in China, etc. Chinese scholars invariably call these ethnic groups 'Dai'. The word Thai, on the other hand, refers to the Thai people in Thailand, who are a part of the Tai ethnic groups in Southeast Asia.

shingle roofs, rather than timber houses with thatched roofs, they still retained a great deal of the Tai cultural traditions and a strong sense of ethnic identity. The village was a typical rice-farming community in the main paddy-growing area of Muang Khon which had begun double-cropping in the late 1960s. Land was increasingly valued because of expanded markets and increased demand for local agricultural products. The introduction of combine-harvesters a decade later resulted in more intensification of land-use and increasing ethnic tensions over landholdings, as the Han Chinese migrants began moving in and laying claim to a share of the village's paddy fields.

But the struggle between ethnic groups in Daikong is not merely a struggle over land, property rights, agricultural products and cash income. It is also a struggle over the appropriation of symbols, a struggle over how the past and present shall be understood and represented, a struggle to identify causes and assess blame, a contentious effort to give meaning to local history and ethnic identity. This book is an attempt to present an ethnographic account of how a sense of Tai ethnic identity is situationally reconstructed and reproduced in Daikong.

To conduct a research project in rural China between 1997 and 1998 and spend another two years at work in libraries and archives is to incur a mountain of debts that can never be fully repaid. I wish to record here my thanks to the villagers of Lak Chang who received me and my family with a courtesy and warmth I shall never forget. The same generosity was displayed by Mr and Mrs Gong Su Zheng, directors of the Tai Association in Daikong, who have taught me a great deal about Tai social life. I am indebted to Dr Sompong Wittayasakpan for his sound advice and to Mr Zhao Hong Yun at the Yunnan Nationalities Research Institute and Mr Ping Long Fang for his assistance in the field.

Thanks are due to my teachers at Berkeley, in particular to Professors Herbert Phillips, George DeVos and William Shack, and to my teachers at Chiang Mai, especially Suthep Sunthornpesuth, Shalardchai Ramitanond and Anan Ganjanapan. I owe a debt of gratitude to my teacher Professor Philip Silverman for many lessons I have learned from him. A special word of thanks goes to Professor Chatthip Nartsupha, whose constant encouragement and support proved invaluable to my research. I am grateful to Professor Shigeharu Tanabe for his critical remarks, questions and suggestions for improvement of the manuscript. Thanks are due to the Thailand Research Fund which provided support for the fieldwork and to Dr Andrew Walker and Dr Nicholas Tapp at The Australian National University. I wish to express my special thanks to Dr Andrew Walker for his kind words and valuable assistance in publishing this book.

Finally, to my parents, my wife and children, who have been with me always, I offer my deepest gratitude.

Yos Santasombat
Chiang Mai
November 2000

INTRODUCTION

The Tai ethnic group, in its different branches, is beyond any doubt one of the most widespread of any ethnic group in the Southeast Asian peninsula. Different branches of the Tai are found from Assam, Vietnam and Laos to the Chinese province of Guangxi, and from Thailand to the interior of Yunnan.[1] In Yunnan province, southern China, there are at least two major centres of the Tai civilisation. One is Sipsongpanna,[2] home of the Tai Lue in southern Yunnan, and another is Daikong,[3] home of the Tai Yai in western Yunnan. While the Tai Lue of Sipsongpanna have been described sketchily by various students of Tai studies,[4] little is known of the Tai Daikong in western Yunnan.

The Tai Daikong are known by various names. They call themselves "Tai Luang" or Tai Yai and in fact share remarkable cultural similarities with the Tai Yai of Shan States[5] and the Tai Yai in Mae Hong Son province of northwest Thailand.[6] According to Chea Yanchong,[7] Tai Daikong refers to a particular group of Tai who settled and continued to live in the areas south (*dai*) of the River Kong (or Salaween). The Chinese scholars have invariably called this group "Tai Dehong", "Tai Mao", or "Tai Nua"; all these different names connote different state names or places of residence. Professor Chea further distinguished Tai Daikong into two distinct groups. The first group is called Tai Nua (northern Tai). This group of Tai Nua lives near the Burma–Chinese border, in the areas of Muang Mao, Muang

---

1 See, for example, Dodd (1923); Eberhardt (1968); Izikowitz (1962); Lebar, et al. (1964); Terwiel, et al. (1990); Condominas (1990).
2 Sipsongpanna is formally called the "Xishuang Banna Dai Autonomous Prefecture" by the Chinese government.
3 Daikong is formally called the "Dehong Dai and Jing Po Nationalities Autonomous Prefecture".
4 See, for example, Anan Ganjanapan (1994); Chea Yanchong (1995); Hsieh Shih-Chung (1989).
5 See Elias (1876); Milne (1910); Leach (1954); Saimong Mangrai (1963); Eberhardt (1988).
6 See Tannenbaum (1982); Durrenberger (1983).
7 Chea Yanchong (1995:34).

Wan Teng or Wan Tieng, Muang One and Chiang Fang. Another group is called "Tai Dai" (southern Tai). The Tai Dai live in the areas of Muang Khon, Muang Ti and Muang La. These two groups of Tai Dehong share many similarities in terms of cultural traits. The spoken languages are basically the same but the written languages are mutually incomprehensible. Tai Dai uses the Tai Pong written characters of the Shan States, while the Tai Nua's written characters resemble those of the Tai Ahom in Assam.

As if the multitude of tribe and state names (e.g. Tai Daikong, Tai Dehong, Tai Mao, Tai Nua, Tai Luang and Tai Yai) are not bewildering and confusing enough, a number of Western scholars[8] have adopted the Burmese term "Shan" and referred to Tai Mao or Tai Daikong as "Chinese Shan", "Mao Shan", or "Shan of Yunnan". In fact, as Leach[9] has noted, the Burmese apply the term "Shan" consistently to all the inhabitants of the Yunnan–Burma frontiers area who call themselves Tai. The Burmese usage of the term "Shan" has not been confined only to Tai Yai but also included other ethnic Tais such as Tai Lue and Tai Khun[10] who speak different dialects.

The question, then, is who are the Tai Daikong? Postulating from the linguistic arguments, around the eighth century AD, the Tai world already extended across much of northern Southeast Asia, differentiated into five linguistic groups.[11] The western group were ancestors of the present Tai Yai in Burma and Yunnan. By the next century, Tai-speaking chieftaincies were established on the flooded plains of the River Mao. These were believed to be Muang Mao and Pong. In the succeeding centuries, the western group of Tai-speaking people established themselves as the governing population through the Burmese Shan states, Assam and in much of Yunnan.

---

8   Elias (1876); Burling (1992:85); Tanabe (1991:44).
9   Leach (1954).
10 Anan (1994:7–9).
11 Wyatt (1984:11–13). According to Wyatt, Tai-speaking people can be differentiated into five groups:
    (1) the northern group, ancestors of Zhuang; (2) Upland Tai group, ancestors of Black, Red and White Tai; (3) Siang Kwang group, ancestors of central Thai (Siamese); (4) Lao group, ancestors of Lao and Sukhothai languages; and (5) Western group, ancestors of Shan, Ahom and Lue languages.

Historical Studies of the Tai Yai: A Brief Sketch

Western studies of Tai Yai ever since the mid-nineteenth century have focused on the historical development of this particular group. Ney Elias's pioneering work on the *History of the Shan in Upper Burma and Western Yunnan* is an attempt to outline Tai Yai history on the basis of Shan chronicles collected in Mandalay such as the Muang Mao, Shweli and Kosampi chronicles.[12] Further attempts to present a brief sketch of the Tai Yai history, such as the works of Scott and Hardiman[13] and Cochrane,[14] are also based on Tai Yai chronicles.

However, the multitude of tribe names and state names and the conflicting dates recorded in these chronicles have led to different interpretations of Tai Yai history. For example, the kingdom of Pong appears in the translation of a Tai Yai chronicle obtained in Manipur by Captain Pemberton in 1895. The same kingdom is mentioned in the list of conquests by Anoratha, the king of Pagan who conquered all the Tai Yai country up to Yunnan and reached Angkor and Lopburi in the early eleventh century. E.H. Parker, by dint of Chinese learning, believed the kingdom of Pong to be Luh-Schwan, while Ney Elias was convinced that it was Muang Mao.[15] Differences in interpretation remind us to treat historical analyses based on the Tai Yai chronicles with caution. Conflicting historical interpretations and debates among Tai scholars concerning the dates and names of a number of Tai Yai states continue to the present.

According to many chronicles, the Tai Yai trace their existence as a nation to the fabulous source of the heaven-descended kings, Khun Lung (or Khun Lu) and Khun Lai.[16] Most Tai Yai chronicles begin with the legend that, in the middle of the sixth century, two brothers, Khun Lung and Khun Lai, descended from heaven and took up their abode in Hsenwi, or in the valley of the Shweli, or of

---

12 Elias (1876:1–4).
13 Scott and Hardiman (1900).
14 Cochrane (1910).
15 Scott and Hardiman (1900:188); cf. Changli (1990:49–60).
16 See Bandit (1994); Chea (1995:33); Sompong (1999:19).

the Irrawaddy. There they found a population which immediately accepted them as kings. Khun Lung and Khun Lai founded Muang Mao or Kawsampi and sent their children to rule over Tai chieftaincies in the plains of the River Mao. Some chronicles state that Muang Mao was founded in BE 1111 (AD 568) while others state that it was founded in BE 1378 (AD 835).

A legend which appears in the Muang Mao chronicles has it that Khun Tueng, son of a Naga princess of the Mao River,[17] was appointed in BE 1305 (AD 762) by the King of Nan Chao to rule over the kingdom of Mao. Another Tai Yai chronicle states that in BE 1720 (AD 1177) Khun Fong Kham was appointed by the King of Talifu to rule over Muang Mao. Later on, the kingdom of Mao expanded its rule and subdued smaller chieftaincies to join together under the name of Muang Mork Khao Mao Luang Kawsampi or Muang Mao Luang Kawsampi.

The Tai Yai chronicles attribute stupendous feats of arms to the Tai Yai from the sixth century onward. Widely scattered through much of what is now the Burma–Yunnan frontiers area by the eleventh century, but apparently best organised and most densely populated in Nam Mao or Shweli Valley, the Tai Yai apparently were temporarily held in check by Anoratha, the king of Pagan. The Muang Mao chronicles[18] state that Anoratha married a daughter of the Mao King (the chronicles give a date equivalent to AD 1057),[19] thereby implying recognition of Pagan's suzerainty. However, the chronicles also state that the Mao King never went to the Pagan court as a true vassal must have done. This, perhaps, implies that the Mao kingdom remained independent.

According to Wyatt,[20] the Hsenwi chronicle pulls the whole Tai world together. It treats the Tai world as a single entity, dotted with innumerable centres in communication with one another, stretching from the Black River valley of northern Vietnam to the Brahmaputra valley of Assam. Wyatt asserted that there is little, if any, evidence that the Tai Yai of the Shweli valley attained anywhere near the expanse of territory that is claimed in the chronicle. It is important, however, that the chronicle preserves a tradition of an open world—an environment in the eleventh and twelfth centuries when the political organisation of the world was not

---

17 Bandit (1994:9).
18 Scott and Hardiman (1900:196).
19 Wyatt (1984:34).
20 Wyatt (1984:33–34).

fixed but was susceptible to the ambitions of any group who dared to challenge the old empires. By the end of the eleventh century, the Tai Yai had certainly become the dominant element in the population of northern Burma and western Yunnan. According to Chea Yanchong,[21] a more reliable history of Tai Yai begins in BE 1797 (AD 1254), a year after Kublai Khan of Mongol descent defeated the kingdom of Talifu. The Chinese chronicle states that the Tai principalities of the Shweli valley became real vassals of the Mongol court. But decades later, Chao Sua Khan Fa, King of Mao, assumed the leadership of the Tai Yai of the Shweli valley. He subdued all the neighbouring principalities and pulled the Tai world together. The Hsenwi chronicles[22] state that Chao Sua Khan Fa marched all the way to Kunming. He defeated the Lao states, Chiang Saen, Sipsong Panna and many other chieftaincies. During his reign, the Mao kingdom grew stronger, stretching its influence in every direction.

Historians, however, have assigned different dates to the reign of Chao Sua Khan Fa. Wyatt, relying more on the Burmese records, believes the reign of Chao Sua Khan Fa to be between 1152–1205 AD, while Chea Yanchong[23] by dint of Chinese and Tai records contends that Chao Sua Khan Fa assumed the leadership of Muang Mao in BE 1879 (AD 1336). During his reign, Chao Sua Khan Fa united all the neighbouring Tai Yai principalities and attacked and subdued Ava, Chiang Rung, Chiang Tung, Chiang Rai, Chiang Saen, Lampang and Lamphun among others. He also sent his brother, Chao Sam Luang Fa, all the way south to what is now the central plain of Thailand.

About AD 1338, a long series of wars began between China and the Mao kingdom, perhaps a direct result of the rise to power of the Mongols in China. Early in 1253, the Mongol armies seized Talifu, the capital of old Nan Chao, and moved eastward to supplant the Sung dynasty and rule the Chinese empire. The more aggressive China of the Mongols was to prove almost immediately to be a very different neighbour to the Tai Yai than Nan Chao had been.[24] For nearly half a century after the fall of Talifu, the Chinese had been in undisputed control of Tali and Yunnan,[25] and were seeking a firmer grip on the Tai Yai principalities in

---

21 Chea (1995:34); cf. Scott and Hardiman (1900:195).
22 Wyatt (1984:34).
23 Chea (1995:34).
24 Wyatt (1984:42).
25 Cochrane (1910:25).

the west by diplomatic and military means. The growing Mao kingdom under the leadership of Chao Sua Khan Fa was certainly seen as a major threat to the assertion of Chinese power in the region.

During 1342–1348 the Imperial Court of the Yuan dynasty launched a series of battles against the Mao kingdom, none of which was decided in favour of either party. Eventually, the Imperial Court decided in favour of more diplomatic means to compel the Mao King to acknowledge himself a vassal of the Chinese court. According to Chinese sources,[26] in 1355, Chao Sua Khan Fa sent his son to the Imperial Court of China in token of homage and, in return, the Yuan dynasty granted Chao Sua Khan Fa the title of "Chao Saen Wi Fa of Lu Chuan kingdom" implying recognition of Muang Mao's suzerainty over neighbouring Tai Yai principalities. Chao Saen Wi Fa is the highest title given by the Chinese Imperial Court to the head of tributary states.[27]

Though Muang Mao and other Tai Yai principalities remained practically independent, the shadow of China hung over them and grew darker with each succeeding year. In 1399, internal disturbances within Yunnan presented the Chinese court with an opportunity to begin a divide-and-rule policy.[28] By means of greater military might, the Mao kingdom was overthrown and divided into smaller principalities. Muang Saen Wi, Muang Yang, Muang Khon and other principalities were annexed and directly governed by the Yunnan province of China.

In 1413, Chao Sua Hom Fa, a grandson of Chao Sua Khan Fa, assumed leadership of the Mao kingdom. According to Ney Elias,[29] Chao Sua Hom Fa reigned for many decades and administered the country so successfully that it enjoyed a state of prosperity it had never before attained. During 1442–1448, however, China again launched massive attacks on the Mao kingdom and completely subdued Muang Mao. It is apparent that from then on Mao glory had departed.

---

26 Chea (1995:35).

27 There are contradictory accounts of Chao Sua Khan Fa's relations with China. Ney Elias, and Cochrane after him, believes that the Chinese expedition to Muang Mao resulted in a disastrous defeat of Chao Sua Khan Fa, who fled to Ava, hotly pursued by the Chinese army. Finding that the Burmese would not protect him, he took poison and died, preferring suicide to the disgrace of capture (see Cochrane 1910:25–26).

28 Chea (1995:36–37).

29 Elias (1876:29).

In place of a solid kingdom, we now have semi-independent principalities. In the sixteenth century, Tai Yai principalities east of the Irrawaddy river became the Shan states and were never free from Burmese control, though from time to time various states gained a nominal independence. The Tai Yai principalities to the east and northeast of Muang Mao were annexed to China and remain part of Yunnan province today.

As mentioned earlier, historical studies of Tai Yai since the mid-nineteenth century have relied heavily on the Shan chronicles. Historical accounts of the Tai Yai presented to the Western reader by Ney Elias (1867), Hallet (1885), Parker (1892), Scott and Hardiman (1900–01) and Cochrane (1910), though rather sketchy, fragmented and at times mingled with mythical discourses, contain useful descriptions of the ancient Tai Yai social and cultural aspects up to the sixteenth century.

In all of Tai Yai history, no period is as tantalisingly dark and unknown as the sixteenth to the eighteenth centuries when the Tai Yai principalities came under Burmese and Chinese control and internal conflicts and battles between these principalities were rampant. Historical studies such as Cochrane (1915) provide brief descriptions of important events in that period, but analysis of Tai Yai social and cultural development in that period is totally lacking.

There are a number of historical studies of Tai Yai in the nineteenth and twentieth centuries. The writings of Mangrai (1965), Taylor (1988) and Renard (1988) rely heavily on British colonial records and focus on the impact of British annexation and subsequent colonial administration on the Shan States. In parallel with this there has been an indigenous development of historical writing among a few Tai Yai scholars who aim to understand the historical development of their own society and culture. These are best exemplified by the works of Yawnghwe (1987) and Sargent (1994).

During the past few decades, growing interest among Tai scholars in the origin of the Tai reflects the quest for cultural roots and a search for comparative materials among other Tai living in different social formations. Historical writings on Tai ethnic groups are best exemplified by the works of Jit (1976), Kajorn (1982), Nithi (1990), Terwiel (1990), Srisak and Sujit (1991), Chattip (1991) and Anan (1995), to name a few.

The Ethnography of Tai Yai in Yunnan

In terms of ethnographic writing, several excellent works on Tai Yai were already published early in this century. Leslie Milne's (1910) pioneering work on the Tai Yai in northern Burma provides detailed descriptions of the Tai Yai family and social life based on personal experiences of spending 15 months in Nam Kham, a small town in north Hsenwi, a few miles from the frontier of Yunnan. Other ethnographic writings on Tai Yai, though rather sketchy and impressionistic, include Hallet (1890), Hillier (1892), Woodthorpe (1896), Scott (1936) and Collis (1938) among others.

Perhaps the first systematic study of Tai Yai in the Western ethnographic tradition was the field research on *pai*-i in the Yunnan border area carried out by T'ien Ju Kang in 1940.[30] At that time, the relative isolation of the region was already being overcome. The war with the Japanese had led to increased political, economic and military contacts between the Chinese and other ethnic groups in the border area. The "Burma Road" which was to ferry supplies overland to aid the Chinese war effort cut through the Shan States region.

From his research in the 1940s, T'ien found the Tai to be most obsessed with the complex and ostentatious religious ceremonies he calls the "Great *pai*".[31] T'ien characterises the *pai* ceremonies as "the most important orientation" for the lives of the Tai people.[32] The *pai* involves pledges by individual householders to contribute substantial gifts to the village temple. In any particular year a number of householders might independently make similar pledges, so that the *pai* ceremonies can be quite elaborate and extensive. The arrangements and activities associated with the *pai* are extended and protracted, involving large numbers of people over lengthy periods and the expenditure of substantial resources. T'ien observes that, despite the "private" nature of the *pai*, the Tai associate the performance with beneficial results which are collectively enjoyed. The sponsorship of a *pai* is the culmination of the aspirations of the whole community.

---

30 T'ien's monograph originally was presented to the London School of Economics for a doctoral degree in anthropology in 1948, but was not published until 1986.

31 In Tai terms, the religious ceremony is called "*poi*" or "*ngarn poi*" which means to make merit by donating generous gifts to the temple.

32 T'ien (1986:111).

Furthermore, the sponsorship of a *pai*, like that of a Melanesian or American Indian potlatch,[33] is a status determinant of great significance. Prestige and power go to the individual householders who contribute substantial gifts and strive to sponsor as many *pai* ceremonies as they can in a lifetime.[34]

T'ien's pioneering work, which focuses on the religious cults of the Tai, also sheds light on how the changing conditions attendant on the building of the Burma Road influenced the Tai life. The rise in contacts with the outside world and economic opportunities had some impact on Tai social life. The unrivalled superiority of the Sawbwa or the elite and the ruling family was being undercut by opportunities for work for the Chinese authorities and by new sources of wealth. Land was increasingly valued because of expanded markets and increased demands for local agricultural products. The changed conditions had altered attitudes toward the *pai* ceremonies. Individuals who had previously expressed an intention to perform a *pai* now used these resources in new forms of investment. While they did not repudiate the ceremonies and expressed a high moral concern for their actions, T'ien believed that the attitude towards religious ceremonies had irreversibly changed.

Another important ethnographic study of the Tai Yai is Edmund Leach's *Political Systems of Highland Burma* (1954). In this study, Leach focuses his attention on the whole region known as the Kachin Hills area in northern Burma, where the Kachin and the Shan populations speak a number of different languages and dialects.

Aside from his major contribution to the growth of anthropological theory, Leach also provides comprehensive ethnographic material on the numerous ethnic groups inhabiting the region, especially the interaction of the Tai Yai or Shan with their upland neighbours. To students of Tai studies, Leach's monograph also raises a perplexing problem of how to conceptualise the category Shan or Tai Yai. As Leach points out, the Shan are territorially scattered, but fairly uniform in culture. Dialect variations between different localities are considerable, but even so, with a few exceptions, all the Tai Yai of northern Burma and western Yunnan speak one language, namely Tai.

Leach believes that a most important criterion of group identity is that all Tai Yai are Buddhists. A second general criterion is that all Tai Yai settlements are

---

33 cf. Drucker (1967:481–493).

34 Ethnographic study carried out by Leshan Tan (1993) confirmed T'ien's observation that religious ceremonies were an important determinant of prestige and power among the Tai Yai in Yunnan.

associated with wet-rice cultivation. Tai settlements occur only along the river valleys or in pockets of level country in the hills. Such settlements are always associated with irrigated paddy land. The third criterion of Tai Yai group identity is that all Tai Yai settlements are members of a Tai feudal state. These three criteria are interdependent. The prosperity that comes from plains of wet paddy cultivation implies Buddhism, which implies membership of a Tai feudal state.[35]

Leach also contends that the original Tai Yai colonisation of the river valleys is in fact a process associated with the maintenance of trade routes from Yunnan to India.[36] Leach believes there is evidence that communications were maintained by establishing a series of small military garrisons at suitable staging posts along the route. These garrisons would have had to maintain themselves and therefore needed to be sited in a terrain suitable for rice cultivation. The settlement thus formed would provide the nucleus of an area of sophisticated culture which would develop in time into a Tai-type petty state.

Leach thus proposes a new theory that the distribution of the Tai Yai settlements in the northeast Burma is not the outcome of some fabulous large-scale military conquest;[37] rather, the distribution of the Tai Yai or Shan settlements is determined by the strategy and economy of trade routes.

Even though this theory is clearly speculative, an important implication of Leach's argument is that the Tai Yai culture is not to be regarded as a complex imported into the area ready-made from somewhere outside as most of the authorities seem to have supposed. It is an indigenous growth resulting from the socio-political and economic interaction of small-scale military colonies with an indigenous hill population over a long period of time.

Another significant study of the Tai Yai is Pattaya Saihoo's (1959) ethnographic survey of the Shan of Burma. This study is an attempt to give a comprehensive and systematic ethnographic account of the Shan of Burma, with the emphasis on the study of institutionalised social relations and the beliefs and values associated with them.

The result of the ethnographic survey shows that the Shan are always found practising wet-rice cultivation in well-irrigated plains and valleys. This makes

---

35 Leach (1954:30).
36 Leach (1954:38–39).
37 For example, the wars with China which forced the Tai to migrate southward.

possible stable residence in one place and gives them a secure economic basis and fair degree of economic prosperity which includes a certain amount of industry and trade. The Shan are a homogenous people with a uniform culture, the characteristics of which are common language, economy, political organisation and religion. They speak a common Tai language, grow rice for their livelihood, have hereditary rulers and are Buddhists.[38]

There are a number of ethnographic accounts of Tai Yai in northwest Thailand. Durrenberger and Tannenbaum[39] studied agriculture and economics in the Tai Yai village of Thongmakhsan in Mae Hong Son province, northwest Thailand. Both scholars have provided valuable insights into the context of Tai Yai agriculture, access to resources and economic processes. Nancy Eberhardt[40] conducted ethnographic research which focuses on religious and cosmological beliefs in Huai Pha, a small Tai Yai village in northwest Thailand.

It is interesting to note here, however, that when one tries to search for a more comprehensive account of the Tai Yai of Yunnan, one finds that there has been a negligible amount of anthropological study up to now. As far as could be ascertained, there is no book about the Tai Yai which, apart from containing the needed information on the identity of the people, their population and distribution, would also tell us of the principles of their social organisation—the social status and role of individuals in society, their social grouping and stratification, kinship and marriage, rule of descent, property ownership and inheritance, political institution and religious beliefs—in other words, all the institutions which provide the framework for their social life and the ideas and beliefs that give meaning to the social relationships.

More importantly, after four centuries of isolation and Chinese domination, questions remain unanswered: Who are the Tai Daikong of Yunnan? What common ground is there between the Tai Daikong and other groups of Tai Yai living in other localities? What differences exist? How do they define their own ethnicity? What is their self-definition of Tai-ness? These questions inevitably lead us to the perplexing relationships between ethnicity and the construction of an "imagined community" among the Tai Yai in Yunnan (Anderson 1983).

---

38 Pattaya (1959:321–326).
39 Durrenberger and Tannenbaum (1990); Tannenbaum (1982)
40 Eberhardt (1988).

Ethnic Identity and the Construction of an Imagined Tai Community

Within the domain of Tai studies, ethnicity is often treated as a primordial given. It has been accepted as dogma that those who speak a particular language form a uniquely definable unit and that this unit of people has always had a particular culture and a particular history. Hence, if we describe the history of a language, we are describing the history of the group of people who now speak that language. It is groups of this sort that are meant by reference to the "races", "tribes" and "ethnic groups" of this region.

To some extent, students of Tai studies during the past decades have followed this conventional classification. Edmund Leach was among the first group of scholars to cast doubt on the validity of the application of linguistic material to determine the history of existing groups.[41] Leach notes that, in the Kachin Hills area where he did his field research, intermarriage between the members of different ethnic groups is very common. He also cautions against confusing linguistic grouping and the ethnic categories that may at different times be associated with it (see also Lehman 1979). Many linguists seem now to have adopted the attitude that historical linguistics will tell us very little about the movements of people in Southeast Asia; and evidence is coming to light that surprisingly indicates not only the rapidity with which communities may change their language, but also the persistence of language in other circumstances.[42]

The perplexing problem of shifting and changing ethnic boundaries among different groups in Southeast Asia has been noted by a number of ethnographers.[43] The region is one of constant shifting of ethnic boundaries, their memberships and markers. Leach[44] notes that any particular individual can be thought of as having a status position in several different social systems at the same time. Lehman[45] similarly claims that entire communities might be faced at

41 Leach (1954:49–50).
42 Wijeyewardene (1990:7).
43 Leach (1954); Lehman (1963); Durrenberger (1990); Tapp (1989), among others.
44 Leach (1954:286–287).
45 Lehman (1967), quoted in Tapp (1989:172).

any time with a *conscious* choice about which ethnic group to belong to. Nicholas Tapp, in his study of the Hmong of northern Thailand, contends that it is useful to regard ethnic identity as an *historical consciousness*. Ethnicity is treated here as a matter of conscious choice. We select our own histories, which are the significant events for us now, isolated from the mass of events which we have truly encountered, and they become real to us. This is the constitution of a significant, or a real history.[46] What matters then is how any ethnic group defines its own ethnicity with reference to its sense of the past, and it is this sense of the past which ethnographers must try to uncover and present.

Ethnicity, then, can no longer be treated as a primordial given. On the contrary, ethnic groups everywhere define themselves, and are defined, by reference to their construction of the past or "real history". We are not dealing with discrete groups which can be neatly packaged under ethnic labels but with a choice of identifications and affiliations that are picked up because they seemed advantageous. The "invention of tradition",[47] the way in which its timelessness may be situationally constructed as a weapon in the clash of social interests, is inherent in all political action. The sudden resurgence of Tai-ness among the Ahom of Assam since the late 1960s;[48] the reproduction and reconstruction of Tai Ahom culture after centuries of assimilation with the Hindus; the attempts to separate Tai Ahom history from the history of the Assamese; and the re-learning of Tai language in schools and private associations, all attest to the role of human agency in actively constructing, perpetuating and transforming values in the interest of building political processes of differentiation and commonality. Amidst increasing conflicts with the Bengali Hindus and other groups of Assamese, the Tai Ahom try to differentiate themselves from the Assamese by redefining their Tai-ness in the vocabulary of history, kinship, home and religious rituals. We are thus witnessing a proliferation of Tai studies among the Tai Ahom, the invention of their "real history", the production of ethnic consciousness and the re-learning of language in creating a unified political identity. The case of the Tai Ahom underlines the fluidity and invention of tradition and the forceful capacity of language to generate an imagined community.[49]

---

46 Tapp (1989:175).
47 Hobsbawm and Ranger (1983).
48 Chattip and Renoo (1995:72); see also Saskia (1996).
49 cf. Anderson (1983).

Even less well understood, however, are the processes by which the nation-states define the ethnicity of their minorities.[50] Are these imagined communities the conscious product of government policies? A number of Thai scholars have noted that the historical development of Tai minorities in Yunnan has been constructed according to the "Chinese plot".[51] The Chinese government has been in a position to influence construction of ethnic identity by assembling historical information about ethnic groups, and sponsoring research which allowed productions of identity to be partly invested in Chinese experts and authorities. Even though the Chinese government has taken on the banner of enlightened pluralism and not suppressed cultural differences in this context, it is clear that this liberal benevolence toward the minority groups still domesticates imaginings, attempting to centralise and manage the domains in which ethnic differences may be legitimately expressed.[52]

Hsieh, in a study of ethnic and political adaptation of the Tai Lue in Yunnan,[53] paints a rather grim picture of the processes by which China defines the ethnicity of her minorities. Hsieh maintains that historical and cultural descriptions of ethnic minorities in China are constructed and standardised in such a way that the productions of identity are heavily invested in the Han authorities. These constructions/creations are shaping a new minority world whose major symbols are in many respects contradictory to the traditional cultural symbols of those ethnic groups. Hence, ethnic pluralism in China means that an ethnic minority has to surrender itself to the ruler. Minority peoples are forced to accept the official constructions and to sacrifice their own traditional symbolism.[54]

However, the ethnic minorities may not simply be passive receptors and conscious product of government policies, as Hsieh seems to suggest. On the contrary, contemporary strategies are more complex, minorities have become politically active and seek self-determination, which begins necessarily with the power of self-definition. Ethnic discourse may be constrained by dominant politico-symbolic constructions and yet contain the possibility of innovation. In the case of the Tai Ahom already mentioned, Saskia[55] informs us of the popularity

---

50 Lilley (1990:178).
51 Rujaya (1994:25).
52 Lilley (1990:178).
53 Hsieh (1989).
54 Hsieh (1989:323–324).
55 Saskia (1996:465).

of books, pamphlets, articles about Tai-Ahom language, religion, history, food habits, names, songs and so on. We are thus witnessing the regaining of control over the production of knowledge—the power of self-definition *par excellence*.

Yet ethnic groups are not completely excluded from the values and practices of nation-states. Long periods of domination may result in an internalisation of alien norms as a form of adaptive strategy of an ethnic group seeking survival in a nation-state. Chea[56] notes that centuries of contact with the Han Chinese have brought about a great deal of change for the Tai Daikong in Yunnan. The Burma Road which cut through the Daikong region led to increased political, economic and military contact between the Chinese and other ethnic groups. The Han Chinese from the interior began to migrate and settle down in Daikong, so much so that they are now the majority of the Daikong population. As such, it is not totally surprising to learn that many aspects of the Tai culture have been influenced by the Han Chinese. Many Tai Daikong now live in wattle-and-daub houses with mud floors and shingled roofs, rather than in timber houses on piles with thatched roofs. Many have adopted the Chinese dress fashion and family names and celebrate Chinese New Year.

Perhaps, the Tai Yai emulation of Han characteristics is not just distorted imitation, but has become, rather, a constitutive element in Tai Yai's lives. Subjectivity is a realm where culture and power are closely intertwined and, as such, we cannot afford to gloss over its intricacies.[57] This means that an important point to be considered in defining what constitutes a Tai ethnic group concerns the nature of its subjective construction.[58] This is deeply rooted in the image of themselves held by individuals, communities and polities, with each of these distinguished from others by the particular historical, social and political contexts. *The ethnic identity of a particular Tai group is thus constructed in a continual process not only by external forces and labelling by outsiders with whom they interact, but also by their own socio-cultural process of creating a self-definition.* The perplexing notion of ethnic group is largely attributable to this imagined construction. Thus ethnic categories can be examined only when we account for the continual processes of ethnic construction, both subjective and externally enforced, and at various levels, while at the same time viewing them together in their historical context.[59]

---

56 Chea (1995:39–42).
57 Lilley (1990:178).
58 DeVos (1976:3–10).
59 Tanabe (1991:3); see also DeVos and Romanucci-Ross (1975).

Scope and Purpose of this Study

Since the late 1960s, there has been an indigenous development of ethnographic writing among Tai scholars who intend to understand their own society and culture. These are exemplified in recent works by Akin (1969), Shalardchai (1984), Anan (1984), Chattip (1984), Chayan (1984) and Yos (1996) among others. A steady development of anthropology in Thailand has accompanied a growing concern with the marginalisation of local peoples and their cultures under the impact of capitalist transformation and globalisation. The work of Thai anthropologists, as Tanabe[60] has noted, has therefore tended from the very beginning to be a sociological praxis that is inseparably associated with the development of their own society and culture.

In recent years, growing interest among Thai scholars in other Tai groups outside Thailand, as exemplified by the works of Bunchop (1983), Chattip and Renoo (1995), Anan (1995), Sompong (1999) and Sumitr (1980) among others, also reflects the commitment underlying their academic practice as well as the search for comparative materials among other Tais living in neighbouring countries.

Implicit in these ethnographic writings is also a search for primordial meaning, an attempt to construct the distant past by studying the geographically distant. The construction/discovery that the Tais too have an authentic culture—just as exotic and primitive as any tribal society in the anthropological literature, that we too have supernatural beliefs, rituals, tales and legends susceptible to structural analysis, all of which can be found in the ordinary life of our Tai neighbours who share with us a common ancestry—represents intellectual movements which are meaningful at present to the Tai nation as a whole.

During the past decade, students of Tai studies have devoted much attention to the origin of the Tai race, the historical development of the Tai states, similarities and differences in languages and dialects, and customs and practices among different groups of Tai in various localities. What is missing are ethnographic accounts of Tais living in different social formations, their kinship systems, economics, politics, rituals, cultivation and everyday life; how they think and feel

60 Tanabe (1991:2–3).

about their lives and their world, and how they define themselves, not only in the present and immediate past, but also potentialities in the future. This study is an attempt to bridge this gap by presenting an ethnographic account of one of the least studied groups of Tai, namely the Tai Daikong or Tai Yai in Yunnan.

This study, then, is an ethnography of a Tai people written from a Tai perspective. It is part of an intellectual movement to reconstruct the Tai cultural roots, to search for a self-definition of Tai-ness, and to provide ground for comparison and generalisation of Tai social experience on the basis of concrete ethnography.

In the following chapters, an ethnographic account of the Tai Daikong will be presented. My concern in this study is to determine the nature of Tai ethnicity among the Tai Daikong: What are the processes by which Tai-ness is defined, and how is the imagined Tai community (if there is one) constructed in relation to a sense of real history and ethnic identity?

It should be emphasised that this study is about one single community and the extent to which it is representative of Tai Daikong as a whole varies greatly depending on the focus of inquiry and the kinds of abstractions involved. While all Tai Yai villages share many obvious characteristics, it is also true that certain differences in social organisation and mood that distinguish Lak Chang village from some neighbouring Tai communities seem to reappear consistently in other parts of Daikong as well. It is hoped that when enough detailed ethnographic studies are available, it should be possible to work out a useful description and generalisation based on sound comparative criteria of Tai ethnic identity.

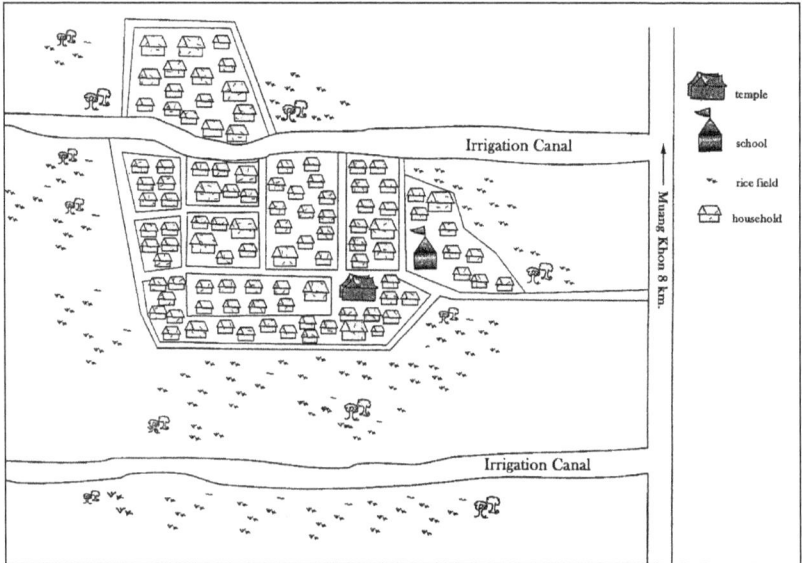

Figure 0.1 Daikong Prefecture and Lak Chang village

Chapter One

THE SETTING

Liu Sam Fong was born 69 years ago in the house his grandfather built. His grandfather was appointed *puu kay* (headman) of the Lak Chang village by the *chaopha* of Muang Khon, so the family house was larger and more substantially built than others. While most Tai houses were built almost entirely of bamboo, his grandfather's house was raised on hardwood piles six feet above the ground. The floor was made of teak wood and the walls of bamboo mats typical of Tai houses. A large open verandah in front of the living quarter was partially shaded by a thatched roof. The interior was divided by bamboo walls into a living room and three small bedrooms. The open space beneath the house served as workroom where paddy was pounded, firewood stored, weaving done, farming tools repaired and chickens, pigs and buffaloes raised.

Sam Fong, like most other villagers, cannot tell with certainty when the Lak Chang village was founded. Some elderly men contended that the village was founded sometime in the fifteenth century when Chao Sua Hom Fah, the King of Mao, was defeated by the Chinese army. The *fang* ruling clan was then granted the *chaopha*-ship of Muang Khon by the Chinese Imperial Court. At the time, there were three tiny villages which had been settled in the area where the Lak Chang village now stands. The *chaopha* of Muang Khon then decreed that these three villages be united and called "Lak Chang" (elephant poles). Lak Chang villagers were thereby ordered to serve as caretakers of the royal elephants.

Mother Nature has been kind to Lak Chang villagers. Flowing down the centre of the valley is the Nam Khon River which has its sources in the mountain ranges northeast of Muang Khon. Small tributaries of the Nam Khon spread all over the great plain of Muang Khon and provide an abundant supply of water all year round. Streams of water which flow through the ricefields of Lak Chang have never run dry in Sam Fong's lifetime.

The great plain of Muang Khon is fertile, water is plentiful and crop yield is great. Vegetable and animal food is abundant. Under normal conditions, every peasant family can produce more rice than is immediately required for the consumption of family members. Life was easy for Sam Fong, that is, until the Communists took over China in 1949.

Daikong and the Chinese Revolution

During the two decades following the revolution, Sam Fong felt the winds of change sweeping over Daikong. Many Tais from Lak Chang and nearby villages fled to Burma in anticipation of social upheaval after the Communist takeover. Sam Fong's wife, Kham, was then pregnant with their second child and the couple decided to stay on and face whatever came their way.

The Communists did not come to Daikong with a specific detailed plan, but they did have an overall perspective. They wanted to advance toward a socialist society, and they wanted to do so quickly. Under Communist rule, Daikong was turned into the "Dehong Dai and Jing Po Nationalities Autonomous Prefecture" and the former Tai feudal states were subsequently divided into five districts: Muang Khon (Mangshi), Muang Ti (Liang He), Muang Wan (Long Chuan), Muang La (Ying Jiang) and Muang Mao (Rui Li).

After liberation, Sam Fong saw a number of young Chinese activists and party cadres come to visit Lak Chang village on a monthly basis. These activists were organised to put on plays, sing songs and give speeches on a variety of messages the Communist regime was trying to convey to the Tai group. Sam Fong heard them tell younger villagers that their *chaopha* was the "oppressor", and remnants of the old feudal state must be destroyed. Then and only then, the villagers were told, could the oppressed peasants be truly liberated. The activists conveyed these messages to students in the village school. Other villagers were encouraged to read certain key works on political theory and government policy and to consider some of the problems that their nation currently faced.

In 1953, the Tai world as Sam Fong knew it came tumbling down when the *chaopha*-ship, the feudal form of the Tai political organisation, was abolished. The royal palaces (*haw*) were condemned by the Chinese government and the various *chaopha*—lords of the sky—no longer retained the forms and appurtenances of royalty, were made district officers and received a salary from the government. "The *chaopha* and the ruling clique had been pursuing personal ends," an activist told Sam Fong, "but now they were to be reformed to serve societal goals." All the land which had traditionally belonged to the *chaopha* was confiscated by the authorities. Sons and grandsons of *chaopha* were sent away either to Kunming or Beijing for further education.

Figure 1.1 The last *chaopha* of Muang Mao who passed away during the Cultural Revolution

Land Reform

In July 1951, district administrators began a broad but superficial survey of the land tenure system in the countryside. They consulted with the village elders and requested them to help develop detailed plans for land reform. Sam Fong still vividly remembers the terrifying uncertainty that all the villagers faced. So many important decisions had to be made, so many people had to work together with new responsibilities and so many circumstances required re-evaluation. The land reform policy was in a constant state of flux and so was the collective sense of security. Many more villagers fled to Burma and those who remained were afraid to oppose the local officials. Each village meeting roused new fears that there would be more disagreements, inconsistencies and changes in policy directives.

From the very beginning, land reform was seen as a political struggle over leadership. In order to swing the balance of political forces in the countryside toward the new regime, the Communists hoped to turn the political tide in the villages by exterminating the traditional status of *chaopha* as lord of the land, by mobilising the peasants to denounce their former ruler in large public meetings and by distributing the land to all peasant households. It was exceedingly difficult, however, for most Tai peasants to attack the *chaopha*. Many local officials, recognising the peasants' reluctance to criticise their former ruler, tried to go lightly on the public meetings and move quickly to distribute the land.

By 1952, the distribution of farmland was completed. Land reform stimulated many new hopes. Every peasant household now controlled the land they cultivated and with only half the villagers remaining home, each household was allocated a large piece of land. Further utopian visions were also drawn for the peasants: rural China was to be mechanised, consumers' needs were to be satisfied and industrialisation was to be achieved in little more than a decade. All the Lak Chang villagers rejoiced. But the celebration of new hopes did not last long.

Once the Communists achieved a firm measure of control over the countryside, a different set of problems and a new vision began to dominate the stage. The problems centred around the economy and increasing productive capacity. The vision was one of an ordered and planned society. This vision was by no means new, but it had remained in the background in the early years of post-liberation when the Communists were scurrying to respond to immediate problems. By

1953, China had begun to stabilise, the problems of governing were under control and government officials had acquired more experience. In 1953, therefore, the Communists turned their full attention to socialist transformation.

In ideal terms, socialist transformation refers to the transfer of economic ownership from private to public hands. In the Communist view, it is conceived as a series of stages in which the scale of ownership gradually expands from smaller to larger collectives or cooperatives until they are fully owned by all the people. During the years 1953–1956, small enterprises and farms all over China were united into "cooperatives" managed and operated by the members who distributed profits among themselves. In 1956, collectivisation of farm land, the prerequisite for socialist transformation, came to Daikong.

Tai Peasants and Cooperative Farming

Despite widespread disagreement about the necessity of socialist transformation and the means for achieving it, most Lak Chang villagers were reluctant to criticise the government. Lak Chang residents took their first step toward cooperative production in April 1956. Attitudes throughout the countryside toward speculation on the one hand and cooperation on the other were undergoing a rapid transformation. The Communists prepared the way by holding "thought preparation" and "rectification" meetings, calling on all the villagers to form trial cooperatives.

A number of village elders remember those meetings well. As one of them put it:

> We had no choice but to jump in and pool our land for joint tillage. We had a lot of land and it was all good. That's why we were worried about our freedom.

In order to ensure that this pioneering effort would start on a sound basis, a work team came from Muang Khon to give advice and help. When the work team first called the members of Lak Chang cooperatives together to discuss the model regulations, they stressed that private landholdings would not disappear. The markers in the fields that divided one plot from another would remain even though peasant members pooled their fields and worked them in common. At this stage, the peasants were not asked to give up the land which their families had cultivated for centuries. Nevertheless, the cooperative still asked them to surrender the essence of ownership, which is the right to decide on use and the exclusive right to the produce of the land.

Many Lak Chang villagers were worried and found it hard to round the corner to socialism.

> All my life I worked for the *chaopha*. He owned the land but it was I who made the decision of what crops to grow and when to do it. But with this cooperative every decision was made for me.

What the villagers found most disturbing about cooperative farming was the work-point system based on a refined concept of piecework that purported to be able to measure objectively the actual amount of work performed by every cooperative member. Linked to this was an accounting system recommended by Soviet experts[1] that in its turn purported to be able to measure objectively the real cost of every facet of the production process.

Right from the beginning, problems and quarrels arose with the work-point system:

> It was a disaster. They gave everything a value and then depreciated everything according to formulas that we found hard to understand or to use. But what was worse, the work-point system threatened to destroy the labour exchange system and mutual-aid groups which had traditionally been an integral part of our production process. We exchanged labour with our relatives, friends and neighbours especially during the transplanting and harvesting times. We also worked together on public projects, with each household sending a member to repair roads and irrigation canals every year. We had our own system.

The work-point system was tried, found distasteful and rather quickly laid aside. But cooperative farming, land and labour pooling remained facts of life for many years to come.

---

1 Cooperative farming and its model regulations did not spring from Chinese experience but were based on the kind of rules and regulations that had long been worked out and applied on the collective farms of the Soviet Union. In the early 1950s, the Chinese made an intense study of Soviet experience and launched earnest attempts to apply what the Soviet comrades recommended. For more detail on this issue, see Vogel (1969:133–136) and Hinton (1983:127–129).

In more ways than one, 1956 was not a good year for Sam Fong. The world as he knew it was crumbling. The crop on his land which he knew so well no longer belonged to him and since it was hard to visualise what any share of the total crop would be, he felt uprooted, cut loose from all past experience, adrift in an uncomfortable limbo, where promises of a socialist utopia could hardly hope to establish full confidence.

The socialist transformation was making his head spin. Mao's Great Leap Forward left him behind in the world of yesteryear. In May 1956, Sam Fong was shocked when he saw with his own eyes how the grand palace was turned into a pile of debris.

I couldn't think it through. It did not make sense. I couldn't understand why they had to destroy such a wonderful work of art, a symbol of traditions which had existed for many centuries.

Unfortunately, the Chinese comrades disagreed with him. The "*haw chaopha*" was the symbol of the old regime, a feudal system that had become anachronistic and had to be wiped away in order to rebuild a new society.

To any younger villagers who would listen, Sam Fong recalled with nostalgia the "free" life of his days under the *chaopha*-ship. He yearned to return to the familiar while he dragged his feet into the new system. His was a community of peasants, family-centred and passionately committed to traditions. The Tai peasants knew of no hunger. The land was fertile and food plentiful. Unlike most of rural China, Lak Chang and other Tai villages never suffered from a severe land tenure problem. The land reform, the cooperative movement and class struggle to overthrow established leadership made very little sense to them.

Since the early 1950s, Sam Fong also saw increasing numbers of Chinese migrants come and settle in Muang Khon, so much so that by 1953 when the first census was taken, the Hans outnumbered the Tai and other ethnic groups and became the majority of Muang Khon and Daikong population (Tables 1.1 and 1.2).

Table 1.1: Tai Population in Daikong 1953–1994[2]

Year	Total Population	Tai Population
1953	402,450	141,100
1955	423,520	138,700[3]
1964	460,665	152,266
1966	503,870	164,500
1967	519,671	168,759
1971	582,214	178,900
1982	749,862	232,327
1985	805,908	252,789
1990	906,426	287,549
1994	952,200	304,700

Table 1.2: Population Census of Muang Khon 1954–1990[4]

Year	Han	Tai	Jingpo	Lisu	Ashang	Palong
1954	51,333	49,680	14,115	1,503	423	2,008
1964	73,143	58,736	12,457	1,147	607	3,385
1982	122,627	87,800	20,179	1,726	1,083	6,116
1990	146,375	107,907	24,945	2,646	1,530	8,153

Before the liberation, there were very limited numbers of Han settlers in Daikong and many of them died of malaria and cholera while the Tai and other ethnic groups seemed to be immune to these diseases. But after the liberation, many Hans were invited to settle in Daikong. The government claimed that they were better educated and should be able to help us develop our community.

Little did Sam Fong know then that there were many more drastic changes and revolutionary upheavals to come. The political pendulum soon swung far to the left as Mao Tse-tung attempted to lay the foundations for a broad united front of hundreds of millions of Chinese from all walks of life, who wanted to get rid of feudal ideology on the one hand, and to free China's economy and culture from imperialist domination on the other.

---

2 Source: The Census Bureau, Dehong Tai and Jing Po Autonomous Prefecture.

3 During the first five to six years after liberation, a number of Tai villagers fled to Burma and Thailand and the Tai population in Daikong decreased.

4 Source: The Census Bureau, Dehong Tai and Jing Po Autonomous Prefecture.

The Commune

On 6 August 1958, Chairman Mao arrived at the Ch'i-li-Ying People's Commune in Honan. The commune had followed the guiding ideas of Mao and was formed by merging together several agricultural cooperatives. It was reported that Chairman Mao was very pleased with what he saw. "It is a cheerful prospect. What a fine thing when the whole province looks like that," he said.[5]

Soon after, three converging movements drastically transformed life in China. First came the sudden and rapid organisation of communes throughout the country, second came a nationwide call for everyone to go out and make iron and steel, third came the growth on local land of an enormous crop, the fruit of hard collective work and very favourable weather. The crop, estimated to be twice as large as any that had been grown before, lifted morale, undercut conservatism and made it possible for large numbers of people to leave home for long periods with ease of mind. As a result, things began to happen at a pace and on a scale that nobody had foreseen.[6]

On 29 August 1958, the Politburo released the "Pei-tai-ho Resolutions on People's Communes" setting forth the basic regulations for the establishment of people's communes on a national scale. Within no time communes were being formed everywhere throughout China.

With food supplied by the mess halls, nurseries and schools supplied for children and resting homes for old people, it was possible for the government to present the communes to the people as an organ designed for their welfare. With the enlarged role of collective life, the expanded size of the collective unit and the increased proportion of goods supplied on the basis of need, the program formed a more coherent picture which could be publicised as progress toward communism, a theme that still evoked a positive utopian image. More importantly, the growth of an enormous crop from the summer harvest made it possible to open the mess halls with generous rations, thus enabling the Communists to portray the virtues of the communes in satisfying the welfare of the people.

The internal logic of the commune, however, was a logic of the hopeful dreamer attempting to impose a vision on less tractable reality. It was assumed that the

---

5 Quoted in Vogel (1969:244).
6 Hinton (1983:214).

masses would be willing to engage in sustained hard work over a long period of time on the basis of ideological and spiritual incentives. It was assumed that people would be willing to work hard even as they turned their own tools and personal possessions over to a higher-order collective. It was assumed that work could be done while differentials in rewards and social status disappeared and the division of labour vastly reduced. It was assumed that local mobilisation was more important than planning and coordination. It was also assumed that agricultural production could be maintained even as many able-bodied men were removed from agriculture.[7]

As elsewhere, the commune campaign in Daikong combined the spirit of traditional festivals with that of militant patriotism. The festival quality was reflected in large rallies, celebrations, parades and music. All propaganda media—newspaper, radio and public meetings—were mobilised to launch the communisation campaign.

Nevertheless, Lak Chang peasants were apprehensive about the commune from the very beginning. Not only did they have to give up private plots and a quota of able-bodied men to work elsewhere, but they had to give up all kinds of private possessions. Family animals, including buffaloes, pigs and chickens, were turned over to the production team. To provide for mess hall facilities and to ensure that people did not have an opportunity to cook on their own, families were asked to give up all their cooking utensils.

Mobilisation for communes disturbed the pace of Lak Chang village life far more drastically than any previous reorganisation campaigns. Cooperatives distributed land and changed the nature of the local work organisation, but the communes penetrated deep into personal life. Not only did many families have relatives living away from home, but those who remained behind had very little time for private lives. Never in the history of Lak Chang, as Sam Fong remembered it, had such large numbers of peasants used so much energy in an effort to comply with a policy they did not fully understand.

Peasant resentment was greatly exacerbated in 1959 when grain production declined precipitously. The increase of land planted with industrial crops, the reassignment of labour power away from agriculture and the gradual dissipation of peasant willingness to work without appreciable material rewards all took their

---

7 Vogel (1969:246).

toll in 1959. Even though Lak Chang did not suffer from the spring drought and the summer floods like many areas in southern China, more food was taken away from Lak Chang and other Tai villages in Daikong to feed the expanding urban population and to provide extra heavy rations for the rural teams sent to work on irrigation and land reclamation. The mess halls were forced to reduce rations. It was the first time in Sam Fong's life that rice was short in Lak Chang.

Cadre commandism was another focus of peasant resentment. The cadres had taken away peasants' belongings and had insisted that people eat in mess halls. They were held responsible by superiors for seeing that peasants worked long hours, that old people took care of the children, that young women worked in the field, that young men stayed at the construction sites, that all farm work was done according to new regulations despite traditional patterns and the shortage of able-bodied men. Cadres could not use material incentives as a leverage for accomplishing these aims and the initial enthusiasm soon subsided with prolonged physical labour, low rations and the lack of free time. Commandism was a problem from the beginning, but it became more serious as the rural cadres were caught between increased pressure for meeting higher quotas and the peasants' growing reluctance to sacrifice without material rewards.[8]

As shortages developed and as cadres became more demanding in their attempts to meet quotas, morale declined sharply. Lak Chang peasants saw little else but confusing orders, emergency tasks, low rations and finally chaos. By the spring of 1959 not only were rations reduced but hard-working peasants were receiving no more than their lazier neighbours. They no longer had any reason to work hard. As the summer crops ripened, more and more people began stealing right out of the fields.

> We took what we considered the fruit of our labour. We could not get anything from the mess halls but a few ounces of watery gruel. If one wanted more food there was only one way—to take it wherever you could find it.

The collapse of the morale of the peasants forced the Communists to initiate a series of measures to reduce the alienation of the peasants from their government. In the winter of 1960–61, the peasants were not only given back portions of their private plots but they were to be compensated for the goods that had been taken from them improperly by the local cadres. Pots, pans, chairs, small agricultural

---

8 cf. Vogel (1969:255).

implements, fruit trees and buildings formerly used by mess halls and work teams were returned to their original owners. If not, the owners were to be remunerated for these possessions as well as for metal belongings taken during the iron and steel drive. Even though compensation was rarely adequate, it was a *sine qua non* for alleviating grievances and getting the cooperation of the peasants.

In Lak Chang, portions of the private plots had been returned to the villagers as early as September 1960. The return of private plots, the reopening of the private market and permission for villagers to keep the harvest from reclaimed land had a great psychological impact. Individual households were also permitted to have their own domestic animals, fruit trees and their own small farm implements. They were permitted to receive cash from the sale of manure and other sideline products.

The acute crisis of 1959–60 was accompanied by a decline of faith in the wisdom of the leaders in Beijing and in the inevitability of economic progress. The collective effort had brought serious failures while the concessions to private capitalism brought moderate improvement. These results caused many to doubt whether progress and communism were inseparable. The success of increased privatism caused many to advocate more concessions to private capitalism.

The crisis of 1959–60 also reflected the deep split within the Party between the Maoist leaders and more moderate—dubbed capitalists—leaders led by Liu Shao-chi and Deng Xiaoping. By 1962, when the conflict had temporarily stabilised and set the economy on an upward curve, Mao moved to stem the precipitous retreat from collective practice that Liu and Deng's emergency measures had initiated on so wide a scale. He moved to block the wind of privatism that was gaining momentum in so many places.

The method chosen was the "socialist education" campaign. The campaign, inaugurated in late 1962, was a determined effort to keep alive a high degree of commitment to China and Chairman Mao, to overcome the tendencies toward privatism and bourgeois selfishness and to initiate an open-door confrontation between right-wing leaders and a fully mobilised people.

The key battleground of the political conflict was over the program for socialist education. The revolutionary zealots who rallied around Chairman Mao wanted a powerful campaign that purged the opposition, mobilised the masses and increased their prestige and power in comparison to that of party bureaucrats. The party bureaucrats, who were practical politicians responsible for running organisations, wanted to blunt the cutting edge of the campaign, to channel it into a harmless educational effort that would curb excesses without disrupting production at their own organisational base. During the course of the next several years, the Maoists succeeded in issuing a number of proclamations pushing the campaign further, but the party bureaucrats succeeded in moderating the effect of the proclamations. Mao turned increasingly to the People's Liberation Army to convey the propaganda message and to provide a power base. As Mao gained more power, the party bureaucrats were forced to make more concessions while seeking new means to subvert the efforts of the Maoist leaders. These conflicts continued to sharpen until they reached high points in the great party purges in 1966–67 and the Cultural Revolution of 1966–76.

Daikong and the Cultural Revolution

In the mid-1960s, Mao became increasingly convinced that the primary obstacle to change and development was the existing party–state apparatus manned by a class of bureaucrats who seemed more likely to lead China to capitalism than to socialism. He believed that the officials in the upper echelons of the party bureaucracy, by virtue of their power and prestige in the state apparatus, were acquiring material privileges and exploiting society as a whole; in effect they were becoming a functional bourgeoisie, albeit one whose privileges derived from political power rather than from property. Mao also believed that an entrenched bureaucracy had acquired a vested interest in preserving the social order over which it ruled and from which it derived its privileged status and thus was opposed to radical social changes and was willing to tolerate and perhaps even actively promote capitalist forms of socio-economic relations and ideologies in China.[9]

This line of thinking placed Mao in direct opposition to most of the other power holders in China and caused him, again and again, to confront the "elite" by appealing directly to the people to launch mass movements that either bypassed the normal procedures approved by economic planners or directly challenged

9 Meisner (1977:354–355).

their expertise and control. The failure of mass movements—such as the Hundred Flowers campaign and the Great Leap Forward—to achieve the goals Mao had set for them led him to a direct confrontation with other power holders in China. When the Socialist Education movement of 1962 also failed to break the capitalists' grip on the Party organisation, Mao launched in 1966 a much bolder and more decisive strategy, a nationwide political offensive that he called a "Cultural Revolution".

The central theme of the Revolution was that the great masses of the Chinese people should rise up, challenge whatever stood in the way of transforming society, enter into lively contention and serious debate, learn by doing and liberate themselves not only from party members in authority who were taking the capitalist road, from bourgeois academic authorities and from cadres guilty of commandism, but also from all the old thoughts, customs, culture and habits of the exploiting class, so as to establish the thought, customs, culture and habits of the working class.[10]

In August 1966, having quietly secured the allegiance of the army and lined up his Cultural Revolution coalition at the apex of the political system, Mao unleashed the Red Guards to attack the party. Most Red Guards were urban high school and college students. Mao encouraged them to "make revolution", "do battle with revisionism", "yank out the small handful of capitalist roaders in the party", "overthrow China's Khruschev", and "destroy the old and establish the new".[11] Red Guard groups quickly launched a reign of terror in most urban areas. They waved the little red book of Mao quotations and engaged in contests to see who could recite the quotations most rapidly from memory. The Red Guards also took to the street to—in the slogan of the day—"destroy the four olds". This translated into destroying old culture by raiding houses, burning books and antiques, beating and humiliating people who seemed not to be in the spirit of things and killing those who tried to resist.[12]

Party cadres at all levels who had immersed themselves too long in urban affairs and isolated themselves too long from the realities of life were sent out to live and work in remote villages. They were supposed to re-establish contact with the masses, do

---

10 Hinton (1983:500).
11 Lieberthal (1995:113).
12 Lieberthal (1995).

manual labour, raise crops and pigs, plough the fields, study politics, repudiate privatism and revisionism, take part in self- and mutual criticism and prepare themselves for the right course of socialist transformation. Those chosen for the honour, however, often found that they had simply been sent away to practise hard labour at a spot so isolated that they could not hope to hold their forces together or ever mount a counterattack on their rivals who had sent them down.

Once the Cultural Revolution began, a drastic escalation of antagonism, both spontaneous and rigged, infected almost all of China. During 1967–68, shocking episodes of increased Red Guard terrorism and violence alternated with more settled times as China shut itself off from the outside world to a remarkable degree.

The Cultural Revolution was extended to Daikong in December 1966. The regional Red Guards were formed in Daikong in early 1967 but the spring of 1968 was perhaps the most violent time, although no firm statistics exist to confirm this. Many Lak Chang elders remembered vividly some of the most shocking episodes of violence that took place in Muang Khon when the *chaopha* and his family became the prime targets of the Cultural Revolution.

> Although the bourgeoisie had been overthrown [the villagers were told] it was still trying to use the old ideas, culture, customs and habits of the exploiting classes to corrupt the masses, capture their minds and endeavour to stage a come-back. The proletariat had to meet head-on every challenge of the bourgeoisie in the ideological field. Our objective was to struggle against the ideology of the bourgeoisie and all other ruling classes, and to transform education, literature and art and all other parts of the superstructure not in correspondence with the socialist economic base so as to facilitate the consolidation and development of socialism.

When these words were translated into practice, however, it meant the torturing and killing of the *chaopha* and his family members, the burning of Buddhist temples and the holy scripts and defrocking of Buddhist monks. As Sam Fong recalled the horror:

> The *chaopha* and his family members were arrested and charged with treason. With their hands tied to their backs the Red Guards paraded them on the streets. They were beaten at intervals and forced to admit that they had been scoundrels all along. No one dared to stop them.

Between 1968 and 1969, the Cultural Revolution inflicted enormous violence on the population and left deep scars and social fissures. Although no reliable figures are available, those in Daikong who suffered incarceration, serious injury or death certainly reached into the hundreds. The *chaopha* of Muang Khon died a few days after his arrest. His wives, children and grandchildren were beaten, humiliated and sent away to do manual labour in the most isolated and desolate parts of the region.

In late 1969, Mao ordered the army to suppress the Red Guards. About eighteen million young radicals were sent to resettle in harsh interior and border regions.[13] The remaining years until 1976 witnessed a see-saw battle between the "moderates" headed by Zhou Enlai and Deng Xiaoping and the "radicals" headed by Mao's wife Jiang Qing. From 1973 to 1976, the moderates generally controlled the executive organs of the political system, while the radicals had the upper hand in the propaganda and media apparatus. The military was not clearly committed and remained an object of concern for both sides. As Mao grew weaker and the succession battle raged, the radicals repeatedly used their control over propaganda machines to stir up mass campaigns to put pressure on the moderates. The rapid changes in policy lines that these campaigns produced exhausted and embittered the population. Politics had more than ever taken a deadly turn and most individuals tried to find ways to weather the storm by silencing and disguising their real thoughts and feelings even more than usual. The Chinese polity had entered a bizarre period of crisis that was brought to an end only by the death of Mao and the arrest, a month later, of the leading radicals who were dubbed "the Gang of Four".[14]

When Deng Xiaoping assumed leadership of the Party in the late 1970s, China began the most far-reaching and systematic reforms that ultimately decentralised political power, energised and changed the ways the economy and society functioned. In the economy, China's real gross national product (GNP) per capita nearly doubled during the first decade of reforms.[15] At the same time, the political system changed in significant ways, with substantial improvements in information flow, policy process and flexibility in adapting to local conditions. China's relations with the international economy and with foreign countries grew

---

13 Bernstein (1977).
14 Lieberthal (1995:118–119).
15 World Bank (1993:186–187).

rapidly. But these changes came at the cost of developing any consensus on national values. The bureaucracy changed little or not at all and thus became more out of touch with an evolving social and economic milieu. Inflation and corruption also became endemic problems.

In the early 1980s, the communes initially formed during the Great Leap Forward were abolished. Instead, China developed a household farming system in which each family leased land from the state. The government eventually permitted leases of fifty years or more. The leasing system provided a means for re-establishing all the incentives of family farming without turning all the land over to direct private ownership. These reforms produced spectacular growth in agricultural output and in peasant standards of living. Peasant demand for consumer goods mushroomed, providing strong market support for increased production in the industrial sector.

Lak Chang Today

During the past two decades, Sam Fong has witnessed a dramatic increase in agricultural productivity, especially in cash crops and vegetables for market. The farmland has once again been allocated to each and every peasant household. The peasants now have greater leeway in deciding which crops to plant and how much of what is grown is sold at free-market rates. Lak Chang villagers' morale has been invigorated. Wealth, prosperity and freedom have once again returned to Lak Chang.

Nowadays, Lak Chang village is home to some 203 households with 962 inhabitants. The village is located about eight kilometres northeast of Muang Khon. The village proper has been enlarged in response to population increases but still retains many of its original features.

Lak Chang village, approximately two kilometres on dirt road off the main highway, can be seen clearly from it across a vista of rice paddies. Each of the paddy fields surrounding Lak Chang is planted at a slightly different time so that the fields ripen in succession, creating a patchwork of iridescent jade and golden greens. Streams of water run from the main irrigation canals and waterways onto the paddy fields. Lak Chang enjoys a semitropical climate with cool, relatively dry winters and a warm, moist summer monsoon season that allows for the planting of crops all year round. Cash crops which are intermixed with the rice paddy fields on a rotating basis include wheat, sugar cane, beans and watermelons. Vegetables such as mustard, tomatoes, cucumber, peas, cabbages, squash and green beans are grown all year round for domestic consumption. All surplus produce is invariably sold at the market in Muang Khon.

Lak Chang village is situated amidst the tranquillity and scenery of the surrounding area. Standing in the ricefield near the village one can see a rim of hazy blue mountains in every direction as one's eye sweeps the horizon. When viewed from a distance, the village stands imposingly above the glittering, lushly green rice paddy.

In spite of the village's scenic surroundings, the layout of the village itself is like that of most Tai villages in this region, rather chaotic with an apparent lack of concern for planning and space utilisation. Dirt roads and narrow alleys zigzag through back corners of haphazardly scattered houses or turn into field paths. Pigsties and outhouses, unaesthetic in sight and odour, block the main thoroughfare in the heart of the village.

Like most Tai villages in the great plain of Muang Khon, the shape or layout of Lak Chang is nucleated: houses are built close together to form a compact settlement cluster. Within the village proper, there is a general absence of green spaces or even space between dwellings. Tight discernible clusters of houses are grouped together in the middle of the ricefields. Lak Chang peasants typically surround their ricefields with groves of bamboo which serve to demarcate Lak Chang from the neighbouring villages.

A small spirit house (*saan chao baan*) stands at the village entrance. Previously, it is reported, every household had a small spirit house made of bamboo with a thatched roof. But today, these spirit houses have all disappeared.

Buddhism, however, is still an integral part of Tai social life. Many Buddhist monasteries in Daikong, including the one in Lak Chang, were burnt down during the Cultural Revolution. Today, a new monastery is being built in the middle of the village. Temple-building has become a major cooperative affair among Lak Chang villagers. All households are called in to "make merit" and to contribute labour and construction materials for the new monastery.

Traditionally, house-building was also a cooperative affair: relatives, friends and neighbours joining to cut bamboo, to weave the wall mats, to make the roof thatch and to erect the house. In earlier days, Tai houses were usually built almost entirely of bamboo. The houses were raised on piles a few feet above the ground to avoid damp and flood. The floor was made of split bamboo and the walls of bamboo mats. The roof was thatched with grass.

Figure 1.2 A traditional Tai house, a style which is rapidly disappearing from the village

Nowadays, however, the architectural character of Lak Chang and other Tai villages in Muang Khon is strikingly similar to the Chinese. The houses are basic in planning organisation and building construction. For the most part, walls are laid out forthrightly in a single rectangular grid. Older homes are of tamped earth construction, with concrete floor and grey-tile roofs. Newer homes are usually built with brick on a foundation of stones taken from the hills nearby. Most residences are constructed around courtyards along the four lateral sides. The single-storeyed main building typically has three rooms, a family room and two bedrooms. The multi-purpose family room serves as a living quarter, a dining room and a memorial hall to honour the ancestors. Here, portraits of ancestors and pictures of family members are hung on the wall above an altar that faces the main entryway. On ceremonial occasions, such as those accompanying mourning or wedding rites, the wooden partitions that separate the rooms are removed to enlarge the space, opening the rooms to the gallery in front. Tradition prescribes that the elder, married brother resides in the east room and younger, unmarried brothers or sisters in the west room with the parents. The kitchen is placed in the eastern wing room as a good omen—following the sun rising from the east, the family itself is to grow. In older homes, a partial second level, generally of wood construction, is sometimes added on the west and the front of the buildings. The resulting loft space is accessible by a steep wooden stairway or a ladder and is used as a granary for rice storage. The ground level is utilised in a number of ways: traditionally, a loom was kept here and, even though weaving has been abandoned, many households still have a loom under the house. The open area also serves as a workroom where farming equipment and firewood are stored and buffaloes and pigs raised.

Most of the village families have wells in their household compounds. Water drawn from the well is used for cooking, drinking and washing dishes. Bathing is done in a flowing waterway or irrigation ditch. Human evacuation is done away from the house and no latrine is found within individual compounds. Public latrines are built overhanging fish ponds, flowing waterways or irrigation ditches running through the village. Young children use any spot at the edge of a waterway as a toilet. Yet village sanitation is good, for the irrigation ditch flows continually and villagers do not use this ditch water for cooking or drinking.

The dress of the Tai in Daikong is fairly uniform in a general sense, but not in detail of colour and pattern which vary in different towns and localities. Today, the man's dress tends to be Western in style, if not in manufacture. Men and boys wear Western-type shorts, trousers, shirts and jackets. These are purchased from the stalls of Chinese merchants in the market of Muang Khon. Loose baggy trousers of Tai origin are still worn by the older men.

Village women, on the other hand, have not completely adopted Western-style clothing. The woman's dress consists of a blouse and a dark-coloured (usually black) *pasin* skirt. This is a piece of long cloth sewn in a tube and folded at the waist and held in place by a belt. Pants and European-type dresses may be found on special occasions among the young unmarried women of the village. But for everyday wear, a blouse and *pasin* skirt can be regarded as the regular costume of Tai women. Married women, however, always wear the characteristic Tai dress: a blouse, a *pasin* skirt and a turban.[16]

---

[16] A turban is an indicator of marital status among Tai women.

A young Tai woman usually lets her hair grow to shoulder length. But once settling down as a married woman, she adopts the hairstyle of the mature women of the community. Married women usually put up their hair in a knot at the back of the head and cover it with a turban. The size and colour of the turban vary greatly in small detail in different parts of Daikong. In Muang Khon, the turban of a young married women is often merely a pink or other light-coloured cotton scarf wrapped around the head. The colour of the turban will become darker as the woman grows older. For field work or for wear to the market town, a soft straw hat with a wide floppy brim is worn on top of the turban and tied under the chin. Apparently, women's dress is still one of the most distinguishing marks of the Tai group in Daikong.

Another distinguishing mark of the Tai is the tattoo. Traditionally, Tai men tattooed their body extensively from the neck to the ankle. The designs and patterns of tattoos were believed to have the effects of charms. Today, most Tai men still have their body tattooed in some isolated parts, especially on the thighs, on the legs down to mid-calf, on the belly, the back or the arms and hands.

During the past two decades, Sam Fong has witnessed a considerable amount of changes in Lak Chang. The market economy is beginning to pervade every corner of social life in the village. Elsewhere in China, the increasing demand for agricultural produce to feed the growing urban population has brought about a sharp increase in the price of farm produce which is a great incentive to production. More and more cash crops are produced directly for the market. The whole process of agricultural production has come under the influence of the market and agricultural productivity has increased tremendously. Increasing productivity has also raised the income of Lak Chang villagers and is beginning to bring about a sharp increase in consumer spending. The village economy has undergone a complete transformation.

With the introduction of electricity in the late 1970s, demand for television sets and other electrical appliances has skyrocketed. Motorisation has also made tremendous progress during the past decade. The construction of new roads has allowed many convenient and novel commodities to flow in. Most peasant households now own a small motorised farm truck which serves as a good facility to transport agricultural produce from the village to the market. The social distance between Lak Chang and Muang Khon has been remarkably diminished because of this transportation development. All kinds of manufactured goods, from soap, toothpaste and cigarettes to motorcycles, have become daily necessities. These changes in consumption patterns mean that most peasant households find themselves in a situation in which more and more cash must be earned and spent to meet the needs of everyday life.

Lak Chang has never been an isolated village; the peasants always considered themselves to be a part of Muang Khon and have always had contacts with the *chaopha* and the market. During the past decade, however, the peasants' contacts with Muang Khon and the outside world have intensified. Every five days, the women take bamboo chopsticks, baskets, bananas, mustards, cabbages, watermelons and other agricultural produce to the open market in Muang Khon. Their motorised farm trucks allow them to buzz over the country roads to Muang Khon in just twenty minutes.

Links to the outside world are also provided by the omnipresent Chinese television sets which transmit events of local and national significance. Increasing links and access to the world outside Lak Chang, however, do not necessarily mean that the peasants are interested in it. Most villagers have only a slight idea of the world beyond Muang Khon. Many of them knew that the *maan tai* (Shan) were fighting against the Burmese army and they knew that there were *pii nong muang thai* (Thai brothers and sisters) who live in Thailand. The villagers' knowledge of the outside world is not increased by their compulsory six-year primary education in the village school. The only language of instruction is Chinese and the school teachers teach mostly by rote learning, which gives no encouragement to originality. The result is that the children emerge from primary school semi-literate at best. They can converse in Chinese but very few can read or write fluently. None of the children continue their education beyond primary school. Worst of all, the Tai written language has not been taught for a few decades and now only a handful of villagers, mostly elderly men, can read or write in Tai. Those who can read seldom do and the village culture is becoming an illiterate culture.

Under four centuries of Chinese domination, the people of Lak Chang and Daikong have been ruled by the authority of Chinese government officials, have been taught Chinese in schools and have been subjected to pressures, directly or indirectly, which tend to acculturate them to the Han culture emanating from

Kunming and to assimilate them into the national Chinese society dominated by the Han Chinese. These forces have had their effect and the village is now definitely a part of China.

Nevertheless, the Tais have not forgotten their ethnic identity, established during the many centuries of their independent existence. The villagers still speak *kham tai* (Tai language), which is intelligible, but with difficulty, to a Thai speaker. The villagers distinguish themselves from the Hans, who serve as government officials over them and who, at times, look down upon the Tais with ill-disguised disdain as "*pai-i*" (barbarians) with uncivilised habits and queer customs.

The villagers view the Chinese, whom they call by the derogatory term "*khay*", with mixed emotions. The Chinese own almost all grocery shops and department stores in Muang Khon and are the middlemen and brokers who collect the peasants' agricultural produce and ship it to Kunming. On the one hand, the Tais admire the industriousness and the business ability of the Chinese. But on the other hand, they are envious of the political power that the Chinese have over them. The Han represent progress, modernity, power and prestige and hold the leading position in the government; and villagers admire them as much as they resent them.

The Tai peasants are also aware of linguistic and cultural differences between themselves and the many ethnic groups, especially Jingpo, Palung, Lisu and Ashang, who live in the mountains surrounding Muang Khon. Their attitude toward these ethnic groups is clouded with an air of confident superiority. A mixed marriage between a Tai and other ethnic groups, including the Han, has never taken place in Lak Chang.[17] "We are a proud people," says Sam Fong, his eyes gazing at the lush green ricefields in front of him, "as proud as a peacock."[18] A proud people they certainly are.

---

17 In the Kachin Hills area where Leach did his field work, he noted that intermarriage between members of different ethnic groups, especially between the Tais (Shan) and Kachins, is very common. This observation, however, does not apply in the case of Tai Daikong. In fact, the Tai are inherently endogamous. This marriage pattern is a result, in part, of the increasing scarcity of land in Tai villages and the ever-present xenophobic antagonism between the Tai and other ethnic groups in Daikong.

18 The peacock is one of the most important cultural symbols of the Tai ethnic group.

Chapter Two

AGRICULTURAL AND ECONOMIC PATTERNS

L ak Chang economy today is clearly a local adaptation of the national economy of China. The latter is essentially a capitalistic market economy modified by state regulatory controls and ownership of key industries. On the surface, Lak Chang, like most Tai villages in Daikong, has grown considerably since the reform of 1976, but it is still a peasant village that has capitalised on its traditional subsistence production. It is important to note that growth in the production system has not resulted in a breakdown of the traditional subsistence production but rather in its augmentation under the influence of the modern national economy.

Yearly Agricultural Cycle

The subsistence base in Lak Chang, as in all Tai villages, is agriculture. The functional unit in these as in almost all economic matters is the family, often referred to as the "household" (*aun*). Goods are produced, distributed and consumed primarily by the household unit and any relevant economic decisions are made there. In Lak Chang, there are 203 such household units, averaging four or five individuals in each. The household is ideally a patrilocal extended family under the leadership of the eldest active male. In the house of Liu, Sam Fong is, therefore, the leader.

Like all Lak Chang villagers, Sam Fong is, first and foremost, a wet-rice cultivator. Non-glutinous rice is his staple food and the main crop. At the beginning of the rice-growing season in late May, his paddy fields, softened by the first monsoon rains of the year, are ploughed by the water buffalo. His plough is made of cast iron with a triangular blade measuring about six inches at the top and tapering to a point, but with a sufficiently large surface. The plough is attached to a wooden yoke fitted onto the buffalo's shoulders and the animal is guided by means of a long string attached to a halter and running through its nostrils.

As the rains increase in frequency, seedlings are grown in a nursery bed which is prepared when the first water begins to reach the fields. Sam Fong selects one of the most fertile fields, on the edge of the village; this seed plot is ploughed and harrowed and the weeds removed. Sam Fong informs his cooperative work group of the day the prepared plot is to be seeded and, on the morning of the designated day, his helpers—about 10–15 people—turn out. Men hoe channels in the soft mud, women follow, scraping up mud with their feet. This work forms eight or ten flat mud beds about three and a half feet wide, separated by foot-wide channels of water. The men then drain the water from the field and Sam Fong's sons walk up and down the rows sowing the rice seed in the soft mud.

Figure 2.1 Irrigation canals in Lak Chang provide an abundant supply of water throughout the year.

The seeds are germinated before they are sown by soaking them for one whole day and then covering them with straw. Water is sprinkled frequently to prevent overheating. Sprouts begin to appear on the second day after they are soaked, and are now ready for planting. They will be allowed to grow a foot or so in height in the seed plot before they are transplanted into the larger fields. A rudimentary bamboo fence is built around the seedbed to keep out ducks and chickens, sometimes scarecrows are placed in the seedbed to chase away birds.

About six weeks later, usually early in June, the fields have been ploughed and harrowed and the seedlings are ready for transplanting. The water flows through the irrigation canals and waterways to flood the paddy fields. Sam Fong's household makes certain preparations in advance; a small straw-thatched shelter is erected near the seedbed to protect the seedlings from the sun after they are pulled and many bundles of thin bamboo strips for tying the seedlings into bundles are also prepared.

Once again, members of his cooperative work group are informed and they gather in the afternoon of the designated day for transplanting. The transplanting group consists mostly of women and transplanting is usually done in the afternoon so that the seedlings will not be exposed to the noon sun on the first day. Seedlings are pulled by the roots and after a few hundred seedlings have been pulled, the bunch is slapped against the foot to rid the roots of any clinging mud. The bunch is tied together with a thin bamboo strip and the tops are usually cut off. The bunches are placed in the shade of the thatched shelter before being transported to the paddy fields, which may be some distance from the seedbeds.

Transplanting usually starts at one end of the field. Both men and women in the work group plant together in a long line, each takes a step about a foot long and at these intervals plant three or four seedlings into the mud. It is tedious, back-breaking work, but is done with a great deal of courting and joking between the sexes. Young men show off by holding contests to see who can finish a row first. Frequent rests are taken to drink tea and smoke cigarettes. When the day is done, Sam Fong invites all members of his work group to an evening meal at his home.

On late June and early July afternoons, Lak Chang is deserted except for old people and small children. Men and women, older boys and girls spend their days in the field and the work will go on until all the village fields have been planted in turn. As they transplant, Lak Chang peasants gradually extend a fresh carpet of evenly trimmed rice lawn across the valley floor. After the fields have been planted, household members can do their own weeding, regulating the water in the household fields and repairing the dikes. The work group will not be necessary again until harvest time four months later.

During the months of June and July, the rain clouds hang heavily over Lak Chang. The rainy season reaches its climax in August, when the Khon River runs swiftly and begins to swell and overflow its banks. By late August, the rains begin to taper off and the rice grows waist-high. The rainy season gives way to winter. The weather begins to turn cold in the early morning and at night.

Harvest begins when plants are yellow and heads droop, showing that the grain is ripe. The average length of time from the preparation of the seedbeds to harvesting is about five months. Harvesting, like transplanting, is a cooperative affair among relatives, friends and neighbours and the work party that helped Sam Fong plant his fields works for him on the harvesting. Each peasant determines the day on which he wishes to start harvesting, but the decision is usually made and the date set in consultation with members of the work group to avoid any conflicts in schedules.

Harvesting time, which begins in October and ends in November, is a rejoicing time when every able-bodied man and woman, armed with a small sickle which has a serrated edge, work together to reap the fruit of their labour. In Lak Chang, water is usually cut off two weeks before harvest time to allow the fields to dry. After that the work group gathers on the appointed day at about nine, after the morning dew has been dried by the sun, and the harvest begins. Once the grain is cut, it must dry in the sun for several days before it can be threshed. In this period, Sam Fong and his children prepare the threshing ground and help to harvest the fields of other members of his work group. When the grain is dried, Sam Fong and his crew return to the fields and tie the rice stalks into clusters of ten with thin strips of split bamboo. About five clusters are tied together to form a bundle or a sheaf. The work crew then beat the sheaves of rice into giant baskets, knocking off the rice grain. The grain is stored in baskets and put away in the household granary.

In Lak Chang, every *mou*[1] of fertile land produces a yield of at least 1,000 to 1,200 kilograms of rice. All peasant households have an average landholding of 10–14 *mou*, so every household can produce much more rice in a single crop than is normally required for domestic consumption. After the paddy is threshed, each peasant family makes an offering to the *chao baan* (village spirits) and gifts of "new" rice are carried to the monastery, with grateful thanks for the blessings of a good harvest.

By mid-November, the harvest is over and the weather begins to turn cold. But winter is not a time of idleness for Sam Fong. On the contrary, this is the time of year when Lak Chang peasants plant crops that supply the money to buy goods and services they themselves do not produce. The raising of secondary crops in the paddy fields and on the other land is an important part of the peasants' activity. Hence November turns out to be the busiest time of year. Right after the harvest of rice is over, the fields are prepared for wheat.

During the Great Leap Forward, Lak Chang villagers were urged to plant wheat as a secondary crop. But the peasants had always considered wheat to be a low-yield crop. Traditionally, they spread whatever compost was available, turned the soil over and sowed seed in rows about a foot apart, then left the crop alone to make whatever heads would grow. Since all wheat was sold at a low price to the government, and wheat was never a part of the Tai diet, the Tai peasants never tried application of fertiliser, careful soil preparation or irrigation on wheat because the yields they expected could not justify such outlays and such effort.

Nowadays, however, Sam Fong and other villagers have realised that wheat, when properly cultivated, is a high-yield crop. Instead of sowing a thin trickle of wheat in rows that are close together, Lak Chang peasants now open up widely spaced furrows at least four inches across and enrich them with fertiliser. They mix organic compost and chemical urea into the soil below, then plant wheat across the whole width of each furrow in a band and bring in irrigation water to drench the whole field. By using the intensive method they learned from the Hans, Lak Chang peasants now reap 30–40 bushels[2] of wheat per *mou*. And the price is very good.

---

1 6 mou = 1acre. This yield seems extraordinarily high household production and is based entirely on the villagers' verbal accounts. However, Lak Chang peasants insisted that a crop of rice normally provides enough yield to last for three years of household consumption.

2 1 bushel = 15 litres.

Soybeans are another important cash crop for Lak Chang villagers. Soybeans grow well in the paddy fields and require no ploughing or tilling. Seeds are normally planted in November in the open space between the dry rice stalks and the ripe vines are cut a week before the New Year celebration in April. Stalks are bound into sheaves which are allowed to dry in the sun for several days before they are threshed. A peasant who has a large crop may thresh his soybeans in the field on a small threshing floor similar to that used to thresh rice. A few baskets of beans are kept for household consumption and the rest are sold by weight to Chinese dealers in Muang Khon. The stalks are piled in a corner of the vegetable garden. After the rains begin in late March and April, mushrooms sprout from the mouldy heap and supply the family with a delightful dish for several months.

In addition to wheat and soybeans, watermelons, onions, garlic, cabbages and groundnuts are also grown in the paddy fields after the rice harvest, partly for domestic consumption, but largely for sale in the market. Numerous other plants are also grown all year round in a garden plot which every household maintains. Various garden vegetables such as tomatoes, chillies, gourds, mustard, potatoes, plantains, ginger and pineapples are grown, both for sale and for home use.

Figure 2.2 Cash crops are intermixed in rice paddy fields on a rotating basis.

Land Tenure

Since agriculture is the basis of livelihood in Lak Chang, land is of utmost importance. Numerous Tai legends concern ancestral heroes who defended their land and fought to the death with the Jingpo and the Lisu and chased them up the hills where they now reside. Lak Chang families now occupy 2,500 *mou* of cultivated land in the immediate vicinity of the village.

Traditionally, the Tai land tenure system was that all farm land was communal property and private ownership was not recognised. The village community, or network of villages, was the land-owning unit and lands were recognised as belonging to one or another village. There were, in a real sense, no landlord or tenant classes in the Tai country. The *chaopha* was the only real landlord in the strict sense when he designated the limits of the land at the disposal of a village. Within these limits, land was allocated by the headman to the villagers according to their needs and the lands might be reallocated at any time to ensure fair distribution or to accommodate new settlers and population increases.[3]

In earlier times, a peasant was allowed to hold only as much land as he could work and as long as he could pay tax to the *chaopha*. Migration, cessation of working the land or expulsion from the village automatically reverted the land to communal property for reallocation by the headman to a new settler or another resident.

In places where the population did not overcrowd the land, the right to work the land passed on to the children after a person's death and the children were allowed to retain the land if they could continue to work it. In Muang Khon, for instance, a greater degree of the right of occupation was recognised. An occupant of the land and his descendants could not be challenged as long as they lived in the village. It was not necessary to work the land to retain the title, inheritance was possible and renting to tenants was also allowed, though not the sale of the land.

The traditional land tenure system was abolished after the revolution of 1949 and was replaced by cooperative farming and, later on, the commune system. After the reform of 1976, however, the traditional land tenure system, albeit in an altered form, was revived.

---

3 cf. Pattaya (1959:162–164).

Of paramount importance at the present time is the basic principle that all farmland belongs to the state and cannot be bought or sold. Farm plots are allocated by an elected village committee to all the households according to their needs and the availability of the land, and the land may be reallocated at any time to ensure fair distribution. Given the overwhelming importance of land allocation in village society, *a central fact of Tai village life today is that there is still sufficient land, that it is evenly and fairly distributed, and that no family is landless or has too little land.*

Since 1976, the paddy land of Lak Chang has been reallocated three times, in 1982, 1986 and 1994. The 203 households of the village now own a total of almost 2,500 *mou* of farm land and the average holding is approximately 13 *mou* per household. In real terms, the communal farmland is officially divided into 203 plots varying in size from 10 to 16 *mou*, depending on the distance of the farmland from the village proper and on the richness of the land. Fields located closer to the village are considered preferable to those further away. Households that are allocated the distant fields usually get a slightly bigger piece of farm land.

The distribution of paddy land is usually carried out according to the needs and the number of people in the household. There is a periodic review of the situation by the village committee so that adjustment and reallocation of farmland can be properly made with regard to the increase in the number of households in the village. For instance, in 1982, Sam Fong, with four sons and five grandchildren in his household, was allocated 16 *mou* of prime paddy land. In the mid-1980s, two of his sons set up their own households and, in 1986, Sam Fong, with only two sons left in his household, was allocated 12 *mou* of paddy land. In 1994, Sam Fong was allocated 11 *mou* of paddy land.

Cooperative Work Groups

In Lak Chang, cooperation is the basic theme of social relationships within the village. "All villagers are *pii nong* (brothers and sisters) and all help one another" is the way village society is fondly described to an outsider. In real life, villagers cooperate in building and keeping up the monastery, and join in communal work to repair the road at the beginning and the end of the rains. They also cooperate in house-building and in cleaning and maintaining the irrigation systems. At weddings and funerals, representatives from almost every village household come to help.

The most outstanding form of economic cooperation in Tai village life is the exchange of labour in rice farming. In Lak Chang, reciprocal work groups help to prepare seedbeds and to plant and harvest the rice. The reciprocal labour-exchange groups are usually activated for rice-growing only, not for growing cash crops like wheat and soybeans.

Every peasant household has its own group of people who come to help and whom it goes to for help. The labour-exchange groups are not necessarily composed of relatives and neighbours, although it is a tendency for households that live close together to work together.

At rice-planting time in late May, the households of a labour-exchange group stagger the sowing of their seedbeds so that the seedlings of each member household will be ready to transplant a few days apart. When the paddy fields have been ploughed and harrowed, word is passed on to the members of the cooperative group that the first household to transplant will do so on a certain day. Each cooperating household then arranges to send the required number of workers on the appointed day to help pull up the seedlings, cut them to an even length and transport them to the larger fields where they are transplanted by the work group. On subsequent days, the other households' fields are transplanted in turn. At harvest time, the same process is repeated as the cooperative work groups go to the fields to cut the rice, thresh and winnow it, and transport it back to the granary of the owners in the village.

The principle of cooperative labour exchange is primarily the number of workers. If Sam Fong's household provides three workers for one of his neighbours at harvest time, his neighbour in turn sends three workers to Sam Fong's fields. Reciprocal obligations are seldom if ever evaded. As a rule, a household must repay the number of labour days it receives from one of the households with whom it exchanges labour. Sam Fong, like all leaders of the household, keeps careful records of these labour transactions. Each morning during the rice-planting season, he will direct members of his household to go help such and such a family to whom labour is owed. Since his household has a number of workers, it is possible for him to divide their labour and send different members to fulfil his obligations to different cooperating households on the same day. If Sam Fong is unable to fulfil his commitment on a certain day, he is expected to hire someone to take their place. During the transplanting and harvesting time, the daily wage is 10 *yuan* per person.[4]

---

4 At the time of field research, 1 yuan was equal to 4 Thai baht and 6 yuan were equal to one American dollar.

The exchange of labour allows the peasants to carry out the back-breaking work of rice production quickly and joyfully. In the fields, there is a great deal of teasing and joking among friends and relatives. Young unmarried boys and girls take the opportunity to flirt with each other. Cooperative labour exchange turns hard work into a pleasant experience which is looked forward to with anticipation especially by young boys and girls.

The importance of cooperative work groups in Tai village society can hardly be overstated. The size of their particular work group is a matter of concern to all village households. A family is proud and its members' faces beam when 25 to 30 people or more show up to help them with transplanting or harvesting.[5] Such a large network of helpers establishes its status as a family that has achieved a good name in village society and it gives its members a sense of pride and belonging.

The same households within a work group cooperate with each other year after year. Labour-exchange groups are relatively permanent and reflect one of the most important social and economic ties in the village society. Members of labour-exchange groups are not only kinsmen, friends and neighbours but also allies upon whom one depends in all important affairs of life.

Animal Raising

The care of farm animals is an important part of Tai peasant economic life. Almost every Tai peasant has at least one water buffalo which is essential for ploughing and harrowing. Water buffaloes are normally stabled in the house compound. Since the paddy fields are cultivated all year round, the buffalo cannot graze in the fields, so the peasant must go out every day and cut grass from the edges of his ricefields and along the irrigation canals and waterways. Buffaloes are raised solely as work animals and they are never slaughtered. Tai peasants normally eat pork, purchased in the village. They rarely eat beef. Milk is also not a part of the Tai peasant's diet and there is no dairy farming by Tai peasants.

Pigs, on the other hand, are raised both for household consumption and for sale in the market. Pigsties can be found in every household compound and pig breeding is a major source of revenue for the villagers. Taking care of the pigs is mostly

---

5 cf. Potter (1976:183–187).

women's work. They are usually fed messes of coarse vegetables and weeds collected from the edges of the ricefields, mixed with rice chaff and all kinds of left-overs, and cooked in a large pot over an outdoor fire; usually enough of this mess is cooked at a time to feed the animals for a couple of days. Normally, there is an average of four to five pigs per family in Lak Chang. Villagers dispose of their pigs, when fully grown, by selling them by weight to dealers who come to the village.

Nearly every peasant household in Lak Chang also raises some poultry. Chickens are raised primarily to sell at the market. Few Tai families eat more than three to four chickens a year and eggs are also rarely eaten by the family. Chickens must forage for much of their food, even though at times they are fed some paddy and rice-mill leavings. Many households also raise a few ducks. The duck is a useful means of controlling pests in the ricefields. A line of ducks waddling along an irrigation ditch early in the morning in the rice-growing season on their way to the ricefields is a familiar sight. They feed on rice crabs, insects and snails that infest the fields.

Non-Agricultural Production

In Lak Chang, some domestic handicrafts are still important, although in the last two decades, many handicrafts have dwindled. Spinning and weaving have all but vanished. Cotton-weaving used to be an important home-industry of every household until cheap textiles replaced much of it. Looms and spinning wheels, at which women worked during the day when free from other household chores, were traditionally kept in the open space underneath the granary. Some of the traditional Tai fabrics are very beautiful; the background of the cloth is usually of black cotton, but it can hardly be seen for the elaborate patterns—woven in silks of artistic shades—with which it is covered.[6] The day of cloth weaving, however, is gone for most village women. All cloth, including ornamental pieces, is purchased from the market.

Tai men have always woven baskets and mats. Today, weaving with cane, bamboo or straw fibre is almost completely in the hands of men. Basket and hat weaving is a more specialised skill practised only by expert weavers, usually older men. Even

---

6 Milne (1910:170–171).

though most handicraft products are largely for home use, many small household items such as bamboo chopsticks, brooms, hats and baskets are additional sources of income for many village households.

Trading is another important part of the Tai economy. Trading at the market place, as part of social and economic life, has taken place for as long as people can remember and, today, markets are held in all large cities in Daikong usually at five-day intervals. In Muang Khon, where Lak Chang villagers go to attend the market and to exchange local news, local traders and villagers from all ethnic groups—especially the Hans, Tais and Jingpos—display their produce and wares in the stalls and on the footpaths. Tai women take a more active role than men in trading. Village women bring eggs, vegetables, fruit, handicrafts and many other items to sell. Traditionally, all trading was done by barter, but today cash transactions are preferred. Most Tais sell their products at the market only to buy immediately some other things they want to take home such as salt, cigarettes, clothes, hoes, knives and other farm implements.

Household Income and Expenditure

The households of Lak Chang are well integrated in the market economy. On average, over 80 per cent of the total agricultural production is sold and only 20 per cent is retained for home consumption. Average household incomes vary very little in Lak Chang, since farm sizes and agricultural production are rather similar for most if not all households. Annual household cash incomes concentrate in the 12,000 to 15,000 *yuan* range.

In Lak Chang, the sale of agricultural produce includes rice, wheat, soybeans, watermelons, vegetables and pigs. Although most peasants produce rice primarily for domestic consumption, the sale of excess rice has always been a major source of household income. The sale of rice is usually done during two periods of the year. The first period is right after the harvest in November. Lak Chang peasants usually sell the "left-over" rice from the previous year to clear their rice granary for storage of this year's harvest. The second period is in July and August when the rice stock elsewhere in China is decreasing and the market price of rice is relatively high. The peasants who have more rice than they need for consumption can get a good price for their crop at this time of year.

Second to rice is wheat, which is the most important cash crop in Lak Chang. Wheat is harvested in March and around this time Chinese traders from Muang Khon and Kunming will bring trucks into the village to buy wheat. When the price is agreed upon, the wheat will be measured and transported from the fields into town.

In addition to rice and wheat, there are various cash crops such as soybeans, watermelons, cabbages, chillies, mustard and other vegetables which are widely grown in Lak Chang. Most of the crops take only a few months before they can be harvested and sold and the village women will bring these crops to sell in the open market in Muang Khon. In recent years, soybeans and watermelons have become very popular among Lak Chang villagers. The price of these crops is high and Chinese traders will come to buy them at the farms.

Pigs are the only animals that can earn income for the peasants, amounting to no less than 1,000 *yuan* per year. Cash income derived from the sale of chickens and ducks is very small by comparison.

Table 2.1: Estimated Farm Costs and Cash Income (yuan)

Costs:	
Seed	43
Fertiliser	250
Insecticide	136
Transport	560
Equipment	180
Miscellaneous	200
Total estimated costs	*1,369*
Income:	
Rice	5,000
Wheat	4,000
Watermelons	1,200
Soybeans	700
Pigs	1,000
Vegetables	800
Total estimated income	*12,700*

Table 2.1 shows estimates of the costs of producing major crops and the farm income per annum. It should be realised that the figures are those of the farmers whose conception of cost is the cash expense incurred in direct crop production. This cost obviously does not include the unpaid wage for family members, and allowance for depreciation of farm equipment and tools, which are usually included in the calculation of cost in ordinary business practice. Another important point is that the reported cost includes only items that the farmers remember and the figure might be slightly lower than that of the actual costs.

Table 2.2: Estimated Household Expenditure (yuan)

Food	800
Clothing	2,500
Cigarettes and liquor	1,100
Health and hygiene	900
Charity and ceremonies	1,400
Total estimated expenditure	*6,700*

Table 2.2 shows the average household expenditure in Lak Chang. Household expenditures include all costs that are not directly related to farming. All peasant households manage to keep their spending below their incomes. In Lak Chang, the costs for purchased food account for only 15 per cent of the total household expenditure. A great deal more money is spent on cloth, liquor and cigarettes. Another major item of expenditure is charity and ceremonies. This includes money donated to the village monastery on special occasions, villagers' contributions to religious activities, contributions made to friends, neighbours and relatives for wedding and funeral rites.

Compared to manual labourers in Muang Khon,[7] all Lak Chang peasants are well-to-do. The surplus of income over expenditure is sufficient to keep traditional agriculture going and for the purchase of a few modern inputs such as farm trucks and colour televisions. The difference between income and household expenditure is saved for house-building and, perhaps, for the most substantial investment of all, that is, the wedding.

---

7 Manual labourers normally earn a monthly salary of 150–200 yuan.

In recent years, Lak Chang villagers put a great deal of their surplus money into new housing and the purchase of consumer goods to improve their quality of life. The new housing they built and the resulting expansion of the village proper took additional acreage out of agricultural production. The population of Lak Chang has also increased substantially during the past two decades.[8] Should the population continue to increase, it can easily be foreseen that the additional population will not be able to make a living on the farmland cultivated today. Agriculture in Daikong is at the crossroads. One can hardly be expected to increase family income and feed more people simultaneously from subsistence production. Even a modernisation of agriculture and an intensification of land use, including animal husbandry, cannot solve both these problems in villages with small farms, which are in a majority in Daikong.

---

8 Even though the Chinese government has, during the past two decades, enforced a strict population control policy whereby a Han family is permitted to have only one child per family and all ethnic minority groups, including the Tai, are allowed only two children per family, Lak Chang's population has only quite recently begun to stabilise.

Chapter Three

KINSHIP AND MARRIAGE IN DAIKONG

The Family and the Village Community

The primary unit in Tai village society is the family household. Basically, this household is a small-family type, which consists of father, mother and children and sometimes grandparents. At times, the family household becomes a small extended family; for example, when a son's wife comes to live in the house and when a child is born to this marriage. Once a young couple have become parents, they usually start a household of their own. Only one son will remain in, and eventually inherit, the family house.

The household is the basic unit of the village community. All village cooperative activities centre around the family household rather than the individuals. The village community is not organised into formal neighbourhood units or divisions,[1] but informal neighbourhood groups do exist for labour exchange in transplanting and harvesting. These groups are determined basically on a geographical basis within the village, for neighbours often work with each other, but the labour-exchange group may also include kin and friends from all parts of the village. Religious ceremonies, temple-building and upkeep, funerals and weddings and repairing of the village roads and irrigation canals are done by the community as a whole.

---

1 cf. Potter (1976:36–47).

Every Tai village is a distinct community; spatially, historically and socio-economically separated from other villages. The people who reside in Lak Chang, for instance, feel a special bond and unity because of their common residence; they speak of "*pii nong* Lak Chang" and identify themselves as brothers and sisters of Lak Chang.

Village unity is enhanced by endogamous marriages. Over 90 per cent of the men and 95 per cent of the women marry within the village. This makes Lak Chang a special kind of kinship unit in which almost every villager is related by consanguineal and affinal ties of diverse kinds. All villagers address each other by appropriate kinship terms. They are grandparents, parents, uncles, aunts, siblings, children and grandchildren to one another, and appropriate behaviour follows the terms of address.

The Tai kinship system is a cognatic system. Descent is reckoned through both parents and every individual is equally related to the relatives of both. Even though the family name comes through the father, who is the head of the family, both maternal and paternal kinsmen are recognised and both are equally related to the family.

Family Relations

In Tai village society, it is morally incumbent upon the young to render esteem and offer homage to their elders. This holds not only for kin, but also for non-kin, and it applies not only to members of different generations but also to age differences within the same generation. Hence, in the Tai address system, the honorifics that precede proper names are systematically age-graded, depending on whether the person addressed is of lower, the same or a higher age-grade than the speaker.

This same attention to absolute and relative age is found in the kinship terminology as well. Generation is a distinctive feature of every kin term. More than that, all kinsmen within the same, the first ascending and the first descending generations are also differentiated according to relative age. Thus, father's elder brother (*lung*) has a different term from father's younger brother (*aah*), older sister (*pii sao* or *pii nang*) has a different term from young sister (*nong sao*) and so on.

The age-graded kinship terms primarily reflect differences in the rights and duties associated with elder and younger kin, which are based on moral obligations. A younger brother, for example, has the moral obligation to pay homage to an elder brother and the elder, in turn, has the moral obligation to care for the younger's children during his absence or after his death. Hence, not only are older and younger brothers designated by different terms, but so are father's elder and younger brothers, and for exactly the same reasons.

In Daikong, as in almost all other societies, the closest ties of biological kinship are those found among the members of the family, the primary relatives of parents, children and siblings. In the family the father occupies the highest position and demands a marked form of respect. For example, the father has his own seat at the dining table and the wife and children who walk past must do so with his or her body politely bent. The position of the mother, on the other hand, is one of affection and tenderness rather than one of authority that demands a rigid form of respectful behaviour.[2]

Though the outward expression of authority should come from the man in his role as the head of the family, in the husband–wife relationship the wife's opinion is often consulted, since Tai women in general have a considerable range of freedom of action and play an important role in economic matters. Men do respect their opinions.

Grandparents by virtue of their seniority demand deference and respect. Their advice and wishes should be followed. To a lesser degree the same holds true with regard to one's elder siblings and other senior kinsmen. There is a strong sense of obligation on the part of children to support and look after their parents in old age. Tai are dutiful children and treat their old parents with kindness and reverence.[3] Grandparents help look after the house and little grandchildren. In return, grandchildren dutifully serve their grandparents when they require help, such as escorting them to the monastery where they may spend their time in peace and quiet, in meditation or in performing religious ceremonies.[4]

In the Tai family, parents are not only the child's most important kinsmen, but also the focal points for the rest of the kinship system. It is the bond with his/her

---

2 cf. Pattaya (1959:202).
3 Milne (1910:76).
4 Milne (1910:87).

parents that forges the child's bonds with other kinsmen, that recruits him/her to membership in labour-exchange groups, and that creates for him/her a network of bilateral kindred.

Figure 3.1 Children in Lak Chang

The parent–child bond is the strongest of all kinship bonds. It should be noted, however, that its strength varies according to the various dyads—father–son, father–daughter, mother–son, mother–daughter—that comprise it. This being the case, family relations within each of these dyads must receive special attention. The focus here, however, is on the cultural norms and expectations that govern these dyadic relationships, rather than on their expression in actual behaviour.

For both parents, the attachment to the son is held to be stronger than to the daughter, a belief that parents generally explain by reference to the son's greater attention to them as they grow older. Daughters, they point out, will eventually get married and leave home. Sons—and their dutiful wives—on the other hand, will care for them when they are old, do their washing, cooking and so on. Regardless of sentiment, this greater attention on the part of the son is culturally constrained by the sexual division of labour on the one hand and by prescriptive institutional arrangements on the other. The latter arrangements not only determine certain forms of parent–son interaction, but are also institutionalised expressions of the cultural conception of, and the normative emphasis on, the strength of the parent–son bond.

For example, there is the custom of newlyweds residing postnuptially with the groom's parents. There is also the custom of the youngest son living permanently with his parents and caring for them until they die.

Despite these cultural conceptions of, and parental expectations concerning, the son, it should be noted in passing that in everyday life the parent–daughter (especially the mother–daughter) bond is very strong. Daughters continue to provide invaluable service to their parents even after their marriage. It is not uncommon for a married daughter to return home and assist her mother at times of illness or during funerals and wedding ceremonies when helping hands are greatly needed.

If the parents' relationship to the son is conceived to be closer than that to the daughter, the relationship of children of both sexes to the mother is thought to be more intimate than that to the father. From earliest childhood, the father is more remote than the mother, and since, normatively, the father is the primary locus of authority, he often engenders a feeling of fear which sometimes persists into adulthood. Although both parents may punish and even beat their young children, fathers do so more frequently and severely. Thus, children and teenagers will seldom go to father when they have a problem or when they are in trouble, for his initial response is expected to take the form of criticism if not punishment. Often, they approach their mother or an aunt or uncle instead and the latter will then broach the matter with the father for them. Sometimes the reluctance to approach the father is extreme,[5] as in the case of Sam Fong's grandson Kong who, when he wished to marry his present wife, asked his mother to speak to his father on his behalf. This, of course, is an extreme case, but even in the more typical cases the child's relationship to the father includes a greater degree of respect and deference than of intimacy and affection.

If the father is viewed more as a figure of authority, one who must be treated with deference, the mother is viewed more as a nurturing figure and a source of

---

5 Milne (1910:76) has also noted a similar reluctance to approach the father among the Tai Yai in Burma, and she made the following observation: "A son who wishes to marry may not inform his father direct, but asks his mother or sister to do so."

affection. The mother–child bond is not only conceived to be stronger than the father–child bond, but, if cultural expressions are to be taken seriously, the mother may be said to be viewed as the pivotal person in the family. The task of child-rearing is thrust solely upon her shoulders and the mother has a great influence on the children. "If the child commits evil," a Tai saying goes, "the mother is to blame." Because of her greater importance to the child, it is believed that a child should not be deprived of his mother. Hence, in the case of divorce (which is very rare), children are allowed to live with the mother only to return to the father's household when they are fully grown.

Although the tie to the mother is held to be an especially close one for children of both sexes, its behavioural expression is particularly evident in the mother–daughter relationship. Even when daughters move out and live with their husbands in separate households, mothers and daughters constantly visit each other. Daughters go to their mothers above all others with their problems, mothers and daughters are close confidants, mothers take care of daughters' children and so on. To care for her daughters' children is the mother's responsibility, but the care of her sons' children, as Sam Fong's wife, Kham, put it, is the responsibility of his wife and her mother. Indeed, the mother–daughter bond is the keystone of the Tai family. Marriage does little to attenuate it and it serves as the chief linkage between households. The mother–daughter bond, as we shall see, also serves as the main source of Tai cultural reproduction and identity formation.

Second in importance only to the parent–child bond is that between siblings. If mutual assistance and aid are normative expectations in all kin relationships, they are especially strong in the sibling relationships. The responsibilities and expectations inherent in the sibling relationship can be differentiated into sex-specific and age-specific responsibilities.

In childhood, the elder sister is important for younger siblings of both sexes and, in adulthood, the elder brother is especially important for the younger sister. In childhood, the elder sister is a surrogate mother for her younger siblings. When mother is absent—when she is busy working in the fields or going to the market—it is the elder sister who cares for them, nurtures them and plays with them. A typical scene in Lak Chang is a young girl, even of seven or eight, carrying a younger sibling on her back, giving him food or preventing him from falling into the waterways. The elder brother, on the other hand, is a surrogate father. He has the moral obligation to watch over his sister and guard her virtue until she is married.

On all accounts, the relationship between siblings of opposite sex is especially close, to some extent they are confidants. The elder brother gives advice to his sister and vice versa. In a sharply segregated society where young men and women (unless they are siblings or cousins) sit at separate tables during a feast and in most social gatherings, the sister plays a crucial role as a matchmaker for her brother. In fact, "no love affairs could commence," as one peasant woman put it, "and no marriages could take place without the assistance of his sister (and/or female cousin) and the blessing of his mother". Since the mother lives with her son in old age, she usually makes her preferred choice of daughter-in-law known to her son. This by no means implies, however, that marriages are fixed and romantic love is reproached. On the contrary, courting is freely allowed in Tai village life. Young men and women have many opportunities to meet discreetly and court in the fields during transplanting and harvesting and on religious ceremonial days or other festivities.

There are, however, important social and cultural constraints on marriage arrangements, if the choice of his marriage partner is deemed undesirable by the mother. For instance, the mother may refuse to talk to the father on his behalf. On all accounts, then, the brother usually consults his sister on this matter and the sister plays a crucial role in the selection of her brother's marriage partner. She approaches the girl he desires and if the girl entertains no fancy for him, she tells his sister directly. As a rule, the initiative for establishing a relationship between a boy and a girl is exclusively the boy's, for however much she may be attracted to a boy, there is no socially approved means by which a girl can take the initiative directly. If a girl likes a boy, she may talk admiringly about him to her girlfriends, with the expectation that they, in turn, will report her feelings to the boy's sister and eventually to the boy. Even the boy seldom attempts to contact the girl directly for fear of being turned down and losing face among his peers. The boy normally approaches the girl through a go-between. Generally, he chooses his sister for this function. His sister then tries to contact the girl and tell the girl of his love, or he may ask her to deliver a love-letter to her. If the girl reciprocates the boy's wish, she may invite him to her house for a visit and the relationship between the two begins from there.

65

The sibling relationship is a special one in Tai social life. Siblings are expected to come to each other's assistance in time of need and to participate in the celebration and commemorations associated with birth, marriage, death and so on. Both physically and financially, the assistance and participation of siblings at a wedding or funeral are all but automatic.

Choice of a Marriage Partner

Marriage is a highly desirable institution in Tai peasant society. In Lak Chang, for instance, only one male (aged 50) and two females (aged 43 and 45) had never married. The small percentage of unmarried adults in Lak Chang is an indicator of the desirability and structural significance of marriage in the Tai social life.

The parents are very concerned that their children make good marriages, boys' mothers, especially, being on the lookout for a good match for their sons. To be sure, the family plays an important role in the initiation of a marriage and in the choice of a marriage partner. Although a marriage can be initiated by the parents, it can be effected only with the consent of the children. What is meant by "parental arrangement" is that the parents—and it is always the boy's parents who make the first move—initiate the negotiations, subject to the approval of the children.

Just as parents will not, and cannot, compel a child to marry against his will, children are similarly loathe to choose a spouse against the parents' will. Parental approval or disapproval of a marriage depends to a large extent on the degree to which the child's choice is consistent with the following criteria, listed in descending order of importance. First of all, it is preferred that the intended spouse should be a Tai. Lak Chang (as well as other Tai village) parents strongly oppose marriage to a non-Tai. In fact, there are no inter-ethnic marriages in Lak Chang. A second preference is that the intended spouse should be a fellow villager. This emphasis on village endogamy is based on several considerations. One does not know a stranger as well as a fellow villager; parents prefer that their child lives close to them after marriage; and finally a stranger is never fully integrated into his spouse's village. A third parental preference in regard to a child's marriage is that the intended spouse should be older than the intended bride by at least two or three years. Tai girls are seldom married before the age of 16 and if they do not fall in love, they often remain unmarried until they are 18 or 20. The average age in Lak Chang is about 18. Men marry at the age of 20 or 22. Aside from important differences in sexual maturation between males and females, a marriage in which the wife is the elder spouse is considered inappropriate because it would cause important confusion in the sex and age respect categories; on the one hand, females are expected to show respect to males but, on the other hand, the younger are expected to show respect to their elders. Preponderantly the ages of spouses in Lak Chang conform to the expected pattern.

Based on the degree of parental approval or disapproval, the Tai classify the ways in which marriage may be contracted into three types: (1) the couple fall in love and the parents happily approve of their children's choice; (2) the parents grudgingly consent to their children's choice; and (3) the parents arrange the marriage with the consent of their children.

When a girl finally agrees to a boy's marriage proposal, he returns to his home and asks his mother to tell his father. If satisfied, his father asks an intermediary— usually an elderly man—to visit the girl's parent in order to discuss the proposed marriage.[6] Should her parents give their consent, the next step is for his parents to approach the girl's parents and discuss the amount of bridewealth. A certain sum of money must be paid by the groom's father to the father of the bride, the amount of money varying according to the "social distance" between the two families.[7] If the groom is a fellow villager, and his father is a close friend of the bride's father, the amount asked—which is not large, usually 15,000 *yuan*—is at first suggested as the price by the father of the girl, but after much bargaining, 10,000 *yuan* may be accepted. The total amount of money must be paid a week before the wedding day. In addition to the money, the father of the groom is expected to contribute a substantial amount of pork and whisky to the bride's father for the wedding feasts.

---

6 The use of an intermediary seems to be a standard practice among many Tai groups, including those in Thailand, as well as in China. See Spiro (1977:180).

7 In earlier times, a ceiling for bridewealth was normally set at 500 yuan by the *chaopha* of Muang Khon, and the bride's father could not ask for more than 500 yuan in exchange for her hand in marriage. But, in recent years, the amount of money paid for bridewealth has been sky-rocketing. A groom's father could pay as much as 12,000 to 20,000 yuan for bridewealth.

Before the date of the wedding can be fixed, the horoscopes of both bride and groom must be carefully studied, many visits being paid to the astrologers or "wise men" of the village.[8] When a propitious day is chosen, invitations are sent by the parents of the young couple to bid their friends and relatives come to the wedding feasts.

The Wedding in Lak Chang

During the third week of our first visit to Lak Chang, the house of Liu was suddenly bursting with activity. Sam Fong's eldest grandson, Kong, was about to get married. Friends and relatives came pouring in to help prepare for the wedding. Unlike their counterparts in the Shan states of Burma,[9] the marriage among the Tai Yai in Daikong takes place with a great amount of ceremony. The wedding feasts are normally held for three consecutive days. All in all, twelve meals are offered to the guests.[10]

In Tai social life, the purpose of the wedding is publicity, in the better sense of the term. It is the announcement of a new relationship in which society—as well as the two families themselves—is interested. For this reason, there is a ceremony, receptions and witnesses. The wedding creates status, rights and opportunity. It gives the couple the opportunity to achieve a new degree of mutuality. The wedding is a major vehicle for the couple's expression of mutual commitment. Therefore, it has a personal as well as a social function.

In theory, the most important participants in a wedding are the bride and groom. But, in reality, the wedding often reflects the dominating personalities or social ambitions of the parents. Exploiting the wedding to serve parental needs is facilitated by the fact that the groom's parents traditionally pay the wedding expenses. In actual practice, the parents are in the middle of wedding preparations, while the young couple remain on the periphery.

For the young couple, the ceremony marks the beginning of a new way of life. Marriage and parenthood both hinge on this event. The wedding can be properly

---

8 cf. Milne (1910:78).

9 cf. Milne (1910:75–84).

10 Tai villagers normally eat four meals a day: breakfast (*kao gon*); lunch (*kao pul*); supper (*kao poi*) and dinner (*kao kum*).

labelled a "rite of passage", for it is the culmination of careful planning, the fulfilment of childhood dreams and the high point in many a girl's life. Though handicapped by the Tai tradition of masculine unemotionalism, the groom, too, often finds his wedding deeply significant.

Although the wedding makes a tremendous difference in the lives of the couple, it marks a turning point for parents as well. When their first child is married, the wedding ends the child-rearing stage and begins the "launching" phase in the cycle of family living. With their last child the launching process is completed.

For parents of the bride, their daughter's marriage is a kind of bereavement. There is a joy of course in the child's happiness. But when she leaves home, a void is left behind, even though the family ties are unbroken. Home is still the place to go for a visit or in times of trouble. After marriage, however, the child shifts her loyalty, her dependence and her home base. As a result, life never looks quite the same again to the parents.

For the groom's parents, the wedding is a major social event and provides an opportunity to create a social display and to make a distinctive impression in village circles. A large wedding should not be a burden that the groom's parents could not readily bear. After all, the family name is at stake. It is the face-saving, prestige-seeking personality that moves Tai villagers to put a great deal of money and effort into organising social festivities. And Kong's wedding was no exception.

A week before the wedding, Kong's parents called on his wife-to-be's parents to discuss the bride-price and the details of the wedding ceremony. The whole wedding process was planned rather in haste since the girl was already pregnant.[11] The bride-price was agreed at 11,000 *yuan*, in addition to 1,050 kilograms of pork and 250 bottles of rice wine.

As the wedding day drew closer, the house of Liu became even more chaotic. Preparation for a wedding involves innumerable details and activities, especially for the groom's household: the furnishing of the bridal chamber, the making of home-brewed rice wine and the preparation of the wedding feasts. Kong's old bedroom was refurnished and turned into the bridal chamber. The bamboo wall that separated his room from the family living room was torn down and replaced

---

11 In recent years, premarital sexual relationships have become more common among the younger generations of Tai villagers. If an unmarried girl is pregnant and the father of the child does not intend to marry her, she is considered disgraced.

with a new one. A new coat of white paint was applied and brand-new red curtaining was hung on all the walls. Kong's uncles were busy with making his new bed. The Tai villagers believe that the bridal chamber must be totally refurnished for the wedded pair. The bed, mattress, bed-sheets, blankets, pillows, coverlet, mosquito net and other bedroom decor should be brand new.

Two days before the wedding, tables, chairs, cooking utensils, rice bowls and other dining paraphernalia were prepared. About 25 tables were set up within the household compound. A temporary fireplace was made in the open air behind the household kitchen and the women of the family, female cousins and relatives gathered round the kitchen and the cooking pots, helping to prepare the food. There was much cooking to be done, and they were to cook almost continuously for three days during the wedding.

The wedding feasts were held separately at the houses of the bride and the groom. Separate invitations were sent by the parents of the couple to their friends and relatives. It was almost as if the entire village was temporarily split into two friendly camps, friends of the bride's and the groom's households, even though in actual practice these two groups had a great deal of overlapping membership.

Guests arrived at the groom's household in the early morning of the wedding day and the first meal of the day was being prepared for them. As the guests entered the groom's household, each made a cash contribution which was used to help defray the expenses. The amount of each contribution was recorded so that the delicately balanced system of reciprocity might be maintained. The guests then proceeded to the household compound and were greeted by the family members. They were invited to sit down and enjoy a sumptuous meal with rice wine. The feasts went on and on from early morning until midnight and guests would come and go as they pleased. Younger villagers, especially friends of the groom who had time to spare, could stay and party all day long.

Early in the evening of the second wedding day, the bride's father sent his "presents" over to the groom's household. It is customary that the bride's father spend at least one-third of the bridewealth buying gifts for the wedded couple. The presents are mostly household items: cooking utensils, mattress, blankets, cupboards, stereo, television set and bicycle. All the gifts were displayed in the middle of the compound so that they could be seen by all the guests. If the gifts are too little, the bride's father will lose face among his fellow villagers.

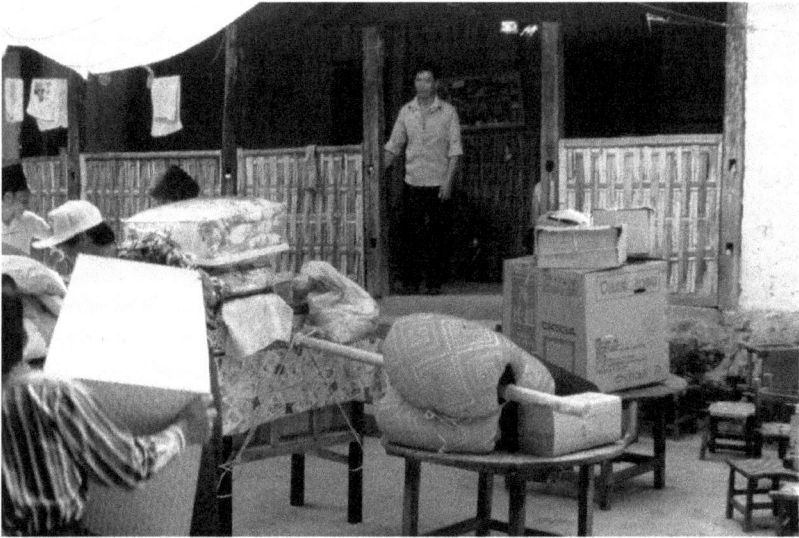

Figure 3.2 Gifts from the bride's father are openly displayed at the groom's house.

At about six o'clock in the evening, the groom's friends came to his home to escort him to the bride. In front of the procession went musicians, with drums, gongs and flutes. After the band came the "escort girls" (*sao hub*) who went to greet the bride and escort her back to the groom's household. Dressed in finest Tai costume, the escort usually consists of two married women and two unmarried ones. After the escort girls came several elderly men, friends of the father of the groom, then the groom and his friends. When they reached the house of the bride, the elders were the first to enter and they asked the bride's parents that she be brought to her husband. The custom is that they should ask for her three times. Twice the father refused the request, saying that he had changed his mind and preferred to keep his daughter a little longer at home; the third time he sent her mother for her. Now the bride had a part to play, and she refused to leave her bedroom. The young married women who were part of the escort girls went to her, begging her to come with them to her husband who was waiting for her. At first she told them to back off, and started to weep bitterly. It is considered correct behaviour for a bride to shed many tears, or at least pretend to do so. At last they persuaded her to go to her father, who placed her hand in the hand of the groom saying, "Here is your wife, you may take her."

The ceremonial fetching of the bride by the groom and his party was now almost over. The procession was on its way back to the groom's household. The band went first as in the former procession. The newly married pair did not walk together: the groom, with his escort girls, preceded by the elderly men, followed the band, then the bride with her escorts. Another set of escort girls (*sao song*)— two young married women and two unmarried ones—was added to the procession. The bride's parents and all her relatives remained in their own home.

There is no special form of dress for bride or groom. Kong, the groom, wore a brand-new, Western-style suit and tie, while his bride was in her finest Tai costume. Her skirt was of black cloth with velvet bands near the foot; the skirt was decorated with panels of woven silks of bright colours. The jacket was of pink coloured silk with a high collar hiding the throat. Her powdered face was covered with red silk and the dangling pearls of her headdress.

Figure 3.3 The bride on her way to the groom's household

When the wedding procession approached the groom's household, they were greeted by a cheering crowd and the loud noise of firecrackers. The groom waited for his bride in front of his house and, when she arrived, he took her hand and led her to the family living room. There, the bride and groom knelt side-by-side facing sets of seated village elders, the groom's grandparents and parents. A village elder instructed the couple to worship the elders and the groom's parents, to prostrate themselves before them, to request their formal approval for their marriage, and to beg their forgiveness for any offence they might have dealt them. The parents and the most senior elder signified their approval by saying "*yuu dii gin waan*" (literal translation: live well, eat deliciously) which expressed their hope that health, wealth, longevity and happiness be vouchsafed to the couple.

After the ceremony, the bride was escorted to the bridal chamber. Two red candles were placed on a stool near the bed. The candles were to last out the night. So was the oil lamp under the bed. They were symbols of their long life together. A red silk quilt was spread on the bed. The bride, still in her wedding gown, sat on the edge of the bed, her head bowed a little and waited for the groom. The groom, however, did not see his bride until the small hours of the morning as his friends tried their best to keep him outside the bridal chamber. This was part of the ceremonial obstruction to the completion of the wedding. In addition, the groom was prevented by the bride's party from entering the bridal chamber until they were paid a ransom. It is customary that the groom should overcome all the ceremonial obstructions and complete the wedding by entering the bridal chamber and removing the bride's headdress.[12]

The day after the ceremonial fetching of the bride, the wedding feasts continued for the third day. On this day, the bride, dressed in appropriate costume for a married woman, could appear from time to time to help out in the kitchen, and the guests could get a glimpse of her. For the first time in her life, her long black hair was combed back, knotted into a chignon and covered with a pink turban, the symbol of a married woman. By the end of the third day, the wedding feasts were over.

The Tai wedding is a purely civil contract and in no way a religious function. Monks are never invited nor are they present at the ceremony. The wedding is merely a public announcement of the couple's intention of living together as man and wife. The wedding is nevertheless a very important ceremony in the eyes of the Tai villagers. A marriage which is not a family affair is not a marriage. And a

---

12 A great many wedding symbols—the headdress, the red candles, the lamp, and the firecrackers, to name just a few—have been influenced by the Han Chinese.

girl, despite her upbringing and the prestige of her family, is not respectable if she enters into marriage unauthorised and unrecognised by the families of both sides. For the parents, and especially the girl's parents, elopement is a cause of such intense shame that they will often agree to their daughter's marriage, despite their disapproval of her intended husband, just so she will not elope.

The wedding is also important for other practical and culturally defined functions as well. First, the wedding represents the only unambiguous means of announcing to the village that the couple intend to live together as man and wife. Second, the wedding is the only means of publicly declaring that the parents of the couple have consented to their marriage. As such, the wedding establishes that the couple are truly married, no one can contest the rights of inheritance by which, in the event of death, the property passes, first to the surviving spouse and then to the children. Even more importantly, the wedding represents the only means of establishing a new household and a new membership in the village community. Only by means of a "proper" marriage can a couple and their children be assured of a fair share of farm land which will be allocated to them by the village land committee.

For the parents, the most important culturally defined functions of the wedding are related to the ever-present Tai motives of prestige enhancement. In Tai village society, prestige derived from wealth is directly proportional to the magnitude of conspicuous display, including both conspicuous consumption and conspicuous waste; and there is little doubt that for the groom's parents, at least, the wedding provides an opportunity for significant social display, because it is they who finance the wedding. Thus the cost of a wedding in Lak Chang, a village whose annual average family income is 12,000–15,000 *yuan*, ranged from 25,000 to 30,000 *yuan*.[13] In short the cost of a wedding is twice the annual income of the average village family.[14]

---

13 There are two primary expenses of the wedding: one is the bride-price (approximately 10,000–15,000 *yuan*) and the other is the expense of the wedding feasts (approximately 15,000–20,000 *yuan*).

14 The magnitude of the wedding expenditure is not unique to Tai village society. The wedding is an occasion for conspicuous display of wealth in many societies of south and southeast Asia. Spiro (1977:189) notes that in Burma the cost of a wedding is equal to the annual income of the average village family, and Indian weddings, according to Mandelbaum (1970:115), are often more lavish than the Burmese.

What is impressive about these figures is that the primary expense of the wedding has no relationship to the ceremony itself, but rather to the food offered at the wedding feasts. Since wealth-derived prestige is a function of conspicuous display, the greater the number of guests, the more refined the quality of the food served and, hence, the greater the expense of the wedding feasts, the greater the prestige value of the wedding. By the same token, the greater in number and the more expensive the wedding presents are, the greater the prestige of the bride's parents.

Sex and Marriage

In Tai village society where premarital and extramarital sexual relations are either prohibited or difficult to achieve, sex is one of the most important motivational bases for contracting a marriage. This does not mean that Tais are especially concerned with sex. On the contrary, the Tai villagers, like most other peoples, view sex and marriage as intimately related, sex being one of the prime motives for, and an important ingredient of, marriage.

Most Tais in Lak Chang assert that of all drives the sex drive is the strongest and the most intense. The men admit that the intensity of the sex drive diminishes with age; as people grow older, other drives, first economic and then religious, become stronger. In any event, most Tais, both male and female, agree that sex is a strong drive, although it is one in which a woman has more self-control. Men, on the other hand, have a low threshold for sexual temptation and, if the conditions are propitious, a man will sleep with any woman he can lay his hands on.

The low threshold for sexual temptation among men explains why, in ideal terms, a male and a female are prohibited from being alone together. It is assumed that all men will be sexually tempted if they are alone with a woman. If a man and a woman are seen together, especially at night, it is simply taken for granted that they are sexually attracted to each other. Hence proper women will not be seen with a man outside her village unsupervised by her mother or brother.

Furthermore, there is a strong cultural emphasis on modesty concerning bodily exposure. The Tai consider it shameful to be seen nude, and one of the most impressive feats of young village women is their agility in changing into fresh clothing, after bathing or washing their hair at the village waterways without exposing any part of their body. Modesty concerning bodily exposure does not apply, however, to married women, who are often seen semi-nude when nursing a baby. When the weather is hot, it is not uncommon for elderly women to wear neither turban nor jacket. The upper skirt is sometimes discarded and the under skirt is tied very tightly under the arms by a string which is knotted across the chest. When a Tai woman is working in the field, for instance, she is not ashamed to be seen in this undressed state. Elderly women sometimes work nude to the waist but one rarely sees young women in a semi-nude condition.

In addition, there is also a cultural emphasis on modesty concerning the discussion of sexual matters in mixed company. Although sex is a favourite topic of conversation in unisex associations, and although sexual banter and obscene sexual humour expressed in double entendre are permitted in certain contexts in sexually mixed groups—for instance, at the wedding feasts—serious sexual discussion is never engaged in in the presence of the opposite sex.

It is paradoxical that despite the strong emphasis on modesty concerning the discussion of sexual matters or bodily exposure, Tai cultural values concerning sexual relations are neither puritanical nor restrictive. In ideal terms, premarital sexual behaviour is regulated and virginity, especially in girls, is highly valued. But, in reality, young men and women have a great deal of freedom; and though such freedom rarely tends to promiscuity, premarital sexual relations and pregnancy are not uncommon in Tai villages. Indeed, it is considered quite normal for a young woman to have had several boyfriends. The parents' major concern is for their daughter to avoid giving birth to an illegitimate child.[15] When an unmarried girl is pregnant, the immediate problem at hand is to arrange a marriage between her and the father of the child. If the father is known and does not intend to marry her, she is considered disgraced.

Although the unwed girl's child is not stigmatised, her parents are. Hence the values concerning sexual modesty are transmitted fairly early from mother to daughter and a thorough sexual education is provided to teenage girls. Daughters usually learn from their mothers about the origin of babies, and how to behave and control themselves in front of boys. From early childhood, girls are taught how to behave in a lady-like manner and they are prohibited from using obscenities. Girls freely discuss sexual matters with their mothers, aunts and grandmothers, while boys learn about sexual behaviour from friends and elder brothers.

---

15 Metford (1935:199), quoted in Pattaya (1959:203).

Among the various forms of sexual behaviour, only heterosexuality is found in Lak Chang. Other forms—homosexuality, various perversions and rape—are absent. In general, village sexuality consists of normal heterosexual behaviour, typically with one's spouse. Extramarital sexual activities and adultery[16] are considered grave offences for both men and women.

Family and the Life Cycle

An important culturally defined function of the marriage is to produce offspring. In recent years, the number of children a village family could have is regulated by a strict birth-control policy whereby the Tai, as an ethnic minority group, could have only two children per family. This means, in effect, that the size of the family has become considerably smaller, with an average of four to five persons per family.

Tai villagers firmly believe that children are given as rewards for merit earned by the parents in previous existences. When many children are born in a family, they show that the parents in their previous lives were known for their kindness and charity and for their good deeds among far-away and forgotten generations of men and spirits.[17] On the contrary, to have no children is a very deplorable state. It signifies that either husband or wife, or both, has been sadly lacking in merit in previous existences. The baby is a sign of moral respectability, a proof of excellence of the past lives of the parents.[18]

Therefore when a baby is born it receives a warm welcome in a Tai home. An ideal Tai family today consists of the parents and two children, a boy and a girl. A boy brings more gladness into the family than a girl, as all Tai believe that a man stands on a higher stage of existence than a woman, and a son is expected to

---

16 Adultery is very rare in Tai village society. According to one village elder I interviewed, there had been only one known adultery case in Lak Chang during the past several decades, one in which the husband was having an affair with the wife of his closest friend. Both were subsequently banished from the village.

17 cf. Milne (1910:31).

18 It is interesting to note here in passing that childless mothers are often instructed by the village elders to make a tiny baby doll, dressed in beautiful costume, and hang it near the Buddha image in the monastery. It is believed that, by so doing, the good spirits who carry the souls of the children to their mothers may see and understand the message.

inherit the family household, carry on the family name and take care of the aging parents in their golden years. A woman, however, also holds an important place in the family and, therefore, a baby girl is also cherished and welcome.[19]

Birth usually takes place in the home. During and immediately after the delivery, the household is filled with female relatives—mother, sisters, nieces—and friends who come to help with the cooking, cleaning and other household chores. During the birth, the husband and all the male relatives are not allowed inside the room. The wife's mother, or an aunt, and a midwife help during the delivery. When a baby is born, she is made to cry by patting or by pouring a little cold water on her head. When she has made her voice heard, her grandmother or her aunt gives her the first bath by pouring warm water over her and rubbing her gently. Then she is dried and dressed. Her little stomach is wrapped with a strip of cloth, and a silk scarf is twisted round her head. A large needle is attached in front of the scarf to ward off bad spirits.

When the mother has rested for a little while her baby is handed to her, and the baby may have her first meal. The mother will afterwards feed the baby at any hour, day or night: whenever she cries, she is fed.

After the baby is born, a fire is lit near the mother and is kept burning day and night in all weathers for 29 days, during which time she is not expected to do any housework, so she has a quiet time to rest and grow strong. Her mother, an aunt or a sister stays with her and helps with the cooking and taking care of the baby. It is also the time when the woman learns the art of mothering from her mother. The practice of *yuu fai* or lying near the fire or "roasting"[20] is common among the Burmese and the Thai[21] as well. In childbirth there is discharge of blood and filthy matter; this is regarded as impure. The purpose of *yuu fai* is thus to *clean*[22] the mother of impurities and perspiration in the body. Lying near the fire is "cleansing with fire", as a village midwife put it, "in order to dry up the things which are impure".

---

19 Indeed, when two boys are born to a Tai mother, she often bemoans the daughter that she is deprived of. A daughterless mother often develops close relationships with her nieces or, later on in life, her granddaughters.

20 cf. Milne (1910:33).

21 cf. Anuman Rajadhon (1961:146).

22 Tai villagers regard childbirth as an impurity. If anyone approaches and witnesses childbirth, he or she is rendered impure. Therefore, a man cannot come within the area for fear that the charms tattooed on his body will lose their efficacy.

While lying near the fire, the young mother undergoes a number of post-partum medical-cum-psychological treatments. Every morning, her mother prepares a medicine ball by pounding salt, tamarind leaves, turmeric and other medicinal herbs, wraps them in a cloth and ties them tightly, forming a ball for massaging. The ball is then dipped in a warm liquid medicine that is mixed and rubbed all over the body, especially the breasts and the nipples. Tai villagers believe that immediately after the birth of a child, the mother's breasts contain hard lumps which hurt and cannot be touched. In order to relieve the pain and facilitate the flow of milk, the lumps must be massaged daily until the pain gradually lessens and disappears.

After massaging with the ball, the young mother's body is pressed with a salt pot. The salt pot is prepared by putting salt into a clay pot covered with a lid and heated until the salt in the pot pops and crackles. The whole pot is then wrapped in a cloth, leaving enough of the ends to gather in a bunch for carrying. The salt pot is then pressed on the young mother's body, especially rolling it over the pubic mound, believing that this practice causes the womb to shrink and return to its "cradle", i.e., to its original position. After the massage, the young mother baths in the liquid medicine and then washes it off with warm water. The entire procedure is repeated daily until she emerges from the fire a month later.

During the whole period of lying near the fire, the young mother is prepared a special diet. Normally she eats boiled rice with salt or dried fish and hot vegetable soup. She is not allowed to have anything cold and must also take special medicine for the blood. Doors and windows in her room must always be kept closed, for it is feared that even a gentle breeze could cause a fever. The susceptibility to fever and cold is said to be due to the fact that the young mother is still weak. Traditional wisdom also has it that bad spirits may slip in through the open doors and windows.

A Tai father plays very little role during the birth of his child and, after the birth, he is asked to perform a simple ceremony of burying the afterbirth, that is, the placenta and the umbilical cord which has been severed by a piece of newly-cut and sharpened bamboo. The afterbirth is washed, rolled in a banana leaf, put in a bamboo cup and buried under a tree. The ceremony is simple and carried out in a pleasant and gentle manner, for this is believed to affect the future temper and well-being of the child. When the father takes the cup containing the afterbirth to bury it, he has a special way of carrying it. For instance, it is believed that the father should shift the cup alternately from left to right, saying that when the child grows up, the child may be ambidextrous. If he carries the cup in only one hand, the child will be handy with only that hand. Burying the afterbirth at the base of a tree is said to be because it is a cool and shady place, and the child will live in happiness and have a long life like a tree. Sometimes Tai villagers bury the afterbirth under the stairway of the house, believing that, by so doing, it will bring more children and prosperity to the family.

The birthday of the child, that is, the day of the week on which he or she was born, is believed to be most essential to the child's happiness in after-life. There are many beliefs connected with this day in many activities throughout the life of the person. Such activities range from house-building, garden planting, business transaction and marriage, to more mundane activities such as hair- and nail-cutting, in all of which the birthday would determine the lucky or unlucky day for the undertaking. For instance, a man born on Saturday should not marry a girl also born on Saturday, otherwise the couple will spend the rest of their lives in poverty and sorrow. The birthday is therefore very important in Tai social life.

After the baby is born, the parents adhere to a strict post-partum sex taboo and sleep in separate rooms for at least a month. When the baby is one month old, there is a ceremonial washing. The parents, the baby, the midwife and other relatives who were present when the child was born, go to a village waterway where the mother washes herself from head to foot, washes her baby and pours water over the hair of her husband and the midwife. The mother is now purified and may assume her conjugal role and household duties.

After the ceremonial washing, a feast is made for the naming of the baby. Parents invite their friends and relatives to be present and the food is prepared by the midwife who helped the mother when the baby was born. When the guests arrive, each drops a little present—a small cash contribution of one to five *yuan*—into a small jar. Then the guests proceed to admire the baby, taking care not to say that the child is beautiful or big, for that might bring bad luck. Instead they make nice little speeches to the parents, saying *"yuu dii gin waan"*—may you and your family live in good health and prosperity. When all the guests have arrived, the village elders pour water over the baby, and the midwife ties white cotton thread round the wrist of the baby. Sometimes, a small coin is pierced and strung on it, with the idea of having tied the prosperity and locked it. The midwife then gives her blessing to the baby, saying *"yuu dii gin waan"*. The mother washes the hands of the midwife and the baby is now ready to receive his name. A village elder ties cotton thread round the baby's wrist, and tells him the name that has been chosen for him, usually by his grandfather or his father.

After the child is named, the midwife or the child's grandmother then shaves the first hair of the child, leaving a clump at the top of the head, saying that it protects the top of the head which is still thin. The hair that is shaved off is placed in a lotus leaf and floated on the water or is thrown away, whichever is convenient. In shaving the first hair, it is customary for the parents to make an offering to the *chao baan* (the village spirits). The naming of the child, the shaving of his hair and the offering to the village spirits are all part of the process whereby the new-born child is registered as a full member of the family and the village.

In later life, a child who suffers many illnesses or accidents may have his or her name changed more than once to puzzle the evil spirits that are tormenting him or her. Some symbolic ceremony is sometimes performed by throwing away the child and finding it again at full moon, by giving it to a visitor who sells it back to the parents or by mock burial.[23] Tai villagers believe that all ills, sickness and accidents come from evil spirits. When a child suffers many illnesses, a village wise man or a diviner may advise that some symbolic ceremony be performed. For instance, the child may be dressed up as one of the opposite sex, the child's name may be changed or the parents may pretend that the child is lost or stolen. If there is no baby to torment, the spirits[24] will certainly be deceived and leave the house.

Tai boys and girls play together and are treated alike until they are five or six years old. From seven to twelve years old children of both sexes begin their formal education at the village school where they are taught reading and writing, arithmetic, geography and Chinese history. Chinese is the only language of instruction.

When they are not at school, children, especially girls, are expected to help with the household chores; they are taught to sweep the floor, clean the house and wash the clothes. Tai children today have been quick to adopt modern-style dress,

---

23 cf. Milne (1910:37–39).

24 Traditional beliefs in evil spirits continue to persist in Tai village society today. For more details on Tai religious beliefs and rituals, see Chapter 5.

which is greatly influenced by the Chinese. Boys now prefer to wear pants, T-shirt and sneakers, while girls wear Western-style dresses of brilliant colours, and when they go out or go to town they wear slacks and shirts instead of their traditional *paa sin.*

After completing the sixth grade, boys and girls—now teenagers—become more and more segregated. Village boys and girls become young men and women between the ages of fifteen and sixteen. Young men and women attain recognised social status in Tai village society. A boy is considered to have reached manhood when he has been tattooed. Until he has enough courage to endure the painful and trying operation, his status is that of a child. Tai men are always tattooed, the traditional norm is to tattoo both legs from waist to knee, the thighs being completely covered with an elaborate design in dark blue. This ornamentation may be continued to the ankles. The backs and chests of boys are seldom tattooed. Tattooing on the legs is chiefly practised as a decoration; it is a sign of manhood, no girl recognises that a youth is a man of marriageable age until his legs show the blue markings. Designs, added from time to time on the arms and shoulders, are charms to ward off evil spirits or accidents. Love-charms are tattooed on the tip of the tongue.

No ceremony marks the passing of childhood into womanhood. A girl becomes a "*saao*" when her body matures enough to be noticed by young men, who validate her new status by starting to flirt with her. A marriageable girl wears no turban but lets her long and shining hair hang loose over her shoulders.

As in all societies that allow young people some choice in relation to their marriage partner, the years of courtship in Tai village society are bittersweet. There is the fun and excitement of the courtship and the eternal flirting, gossiping and teasing. There is also the painful lack of confidence of parental approval. But once two lovers are able to be married, the marriage usually lasts until death do them part. Divorce is rare in Tai village society.

As husband and wife grow old, they spend more time in prayer and meditation. Women in their late 40s cease to wear bright colours; their *paa sin,* blouses and turbans become a uniform black. Old people become caretakers of the houses and small children, and spend much of their spare time at the village temple. Old people normally are active in the religious affairs of the village. They spend more time at the temple in meditation and performing small services in the caretaking of the temple, such as sweeping the floor and arranging flowers at the altar.[25] They also take the leading role in the performances of religious feasts.[26]

Old age confers a distinct social status in Tai village society. Even though old people lead calm and placid lives, they are respected by virtue of their seniority as well as by the wealth of knowledge and wisdom acquired by long years of experience. In fact, the "elders" are the most important leaders in Tai village society. They are present in, and chair, all important religious and social activities, from the naming of the baby, weddings and funerals, to land allocation meetings. Each of these elders has an entourage—members of his family and kinship group—which is the basic structural feature of the Tai village society. To be a Tai villager is to be a member of a family and kin entourage of an elder, whose basic constituents are the family households—the land holding units of the village society. The family households are also residential units in Tai village society which reinforce and are reinforced by ties of cooperation, neighbourliness and political alliance. The family thus remains the cornerstone of the Tai village society in Daikong.

---

25 cf. Milne (1910:86–87).
26 cf. T'ien (1986:46–48).

Chapter Four

POLITICAL
AND SOCIAL
ORGANISATIONS

Traditionally, the largest political unit of the Tai Yai in the Burma–Yunnan frontiers was the "state" or "*muang*", which had a territorial limit and was governed by a *chaopha* (prince).[1] Before the Shan country in Burma was annexed to Great Britain in 1886 each *chaopha* governed his own state, and the King of Upper Burma was his overlord, to whom he was obliged to pay a heavy tribute. Western authors[2] have invariably described the relationships between Tai states in terms of factionalism and constant fighting among themselves. According to Milne:

> Burman officials tyrannised over the Shans, and, owing to heavy and unjust taxation, the people were in a state of perpetual rebellion against their Chiefs; the Chiefs were constantly fighting among themselves, and were also trying to free themselves from the Burman rule. The condition of the country whilst under Burma has been described already in the historical chapter, so it need not be repeated here, but I should like to draw attention to the unhappy state of the people under the invasion of the Kachins, who were slowly but surely taking possession of the hill-country. We read in the Parliamentary Papers for 1859–1876: "The Kachins are a portion of the vast

---

1 Milne (1910:186).
2 For instance, Parker (1893); Milne (1910); and Scott (1936), among others.

hordes of Singphos that inhabit the mountain districts of Northern Assam, and stretch round the north of Burma into Western China. These extend not only all along the northern frontier, but dip down southward wherever the mountain ranges lead them... They have ousted many Shan tribes... and wherever they appear they assume the same character of 'lords of all they can reach', only to be appeased by some form of 'black mail'... They inspire such terror, that in the neighbouring plains no Burman or Shan will venture alone, or even in company, unarmed along the roads within their reach. This state of affairs lasted until the British annexation, and our Government has worked what one might almost call a miracle; for the first time since the beginning of Shan history, peace prevails all over the country."[3]

The imagined political landscape of the Shan described by Milne was perhaps a by-product of the making of modern European self-consciousness.[4] It was part of what Jean and John Comeroff called the "discourses of the imperial imagination".[5] It aimed to construct a mechanism of mastery, an explanatory scheme capable of rationalising British colonialism. For, by portraying the Tai states as a land of "terror" and chaos, we witness the rise of a more and more elaborate model of the relationship of Britain to the Orientals, a relationship of both complementary opposition and inequality, in which the former stood to the latter as civilisation to savagery, saviour to victim, actor to subject. It was a relationship whose very creation implied a historical imperative, a process of interaction through which the wild would be cultivated, the suffering saved and the chaos ordered. Once emancipated and humanity established, the savage would become a fit subject of the British Empire.

The imperial imagination aside, we learn from the Tai chronicles[6] that, throughout history, the Tai political landscape had been characterised by the rise and fall of ambitious and powerful *chaopha*. The political organisation of the entire Burma–Yunnan frontier area had been very unstable. Small autonomous political units had often tended to aggregate into larger systems; large-scale feudal hierarchies had fragmented into smaller ones.[7] There had also been violent and rapid shifts in the

---

3 Milne (1910:186–187).
4 cf. Said (1978); Gates (1986).
5 Jean and John Comeroff (1991:86–87).
6 Nanthasingha (1997).
7 Leach (1954:6).

overall distribution of political power. In Tai history, an ambitious leader was able to extend his sphere of influence and enlarge his territory at the expense of neighbouring *chaopha* whose states were either completely annexed into the conquering state or continued their existence as tributary states to the successful *chaopha*. On the other hand, a large state with a weak ruler was often split up into a number of small independent states ruled by the local heads who either had earlier had their sovereignty held in temporary abeyance, or now acquired royal titles by public recognition of their leadership. Often in the absence of a strong authority or in a time of oppression, local communities struggled to break away from the mother-state, either to become independent with their own rulers or to transfer their allegiance to a more benevolent ruler.[8]

The number and size of the Tai states in Daikong as well as in Shan territory varied a great deal. In general, a state (*muang*) consisted of circles of villages with the *chaopha* residing in the capital village or town, which was usually larger and more populous than any other town or village in the state. A large and powerful state usually consisted of several tributary states, which in turn were divided into circles and villages.

To be a member of a state, a Tai had to recognise the authority of the *chaopha* of that state. Though a state had its territorial limit, and membership of a village was dependent upon the residence in that village and the acceptance of the authority of the village headman appointed by the *chaopha*, state jurisdiction over its members was personal and not territorial. In other words, membership of a state could be acquired or renounced on the principle of giving recognition and allegiance to the *chaopha* in so far as his political protection was effective. In a time of oppression, however, migration to another state was normal. In fact, wholesale migration of an entire village in defiance of a *chaopha*'s authority was not uncommon.[9]

The political organisation in all Tai states in Daikong and in the Shan states of Burma[10] appeared to be similar, though the detail and number of officials may vary according to the sheer size and requirements of individual states. The head of the political organisation with absolute power was the *chaopha*, who ruled from

---

8 Pattaya (1959:110–111).
9 cf. Scott (1936:40–44); Parker (1893:312–326).
10 cf. Scott (1900); Pattaya (1959).

his palace in the capital with the assistance and counsel of the council of ministers (*amat*). The *chaopha* and his ministers constituted the central government of the state. Orders and decrees from the capital concerning governmental affairs, tax collection, corvée and military services were sent to the heads of townships or circles of villages who administered the final detail through the village headmen under their respective command. The township or village circle heads and the village headmen constituted the local government.

The *Chaopha*

In Tai terms, *chaopha* literally means "lord of the sky". Traditionally, the *chaopha* ruled by hereditary right as an absolute monarch having the power of life and death over his subjects. According to Leach,[11] the Tai ideal of a *chaopha* was a monarch who lived apart from the world in his sacred palace. He lived a life of luxury and indolence surrounded by a vast harem of wives and concubines. Practical affairs of the state were delegated to the *amat*. These ministers received no salary but made a lucrative living from official positions.

The good *chaopha* was a man who managed to maintain a luxurious and extravagant court and at the same time keep the rapaciousness of his courtiers within bounds. The *chaopha* maintained the forms and appurtenances of royalty: they had many wives and concubines; they sometimes, perhaps, married their half-sisters; and they had the royal throne and the white umbrella similar to the Kings of Burma.[12]

When addressing a *chaopha* or any member of the royalty, a commoner properly used a respectful expression in every sentence. Only his title was addressed and the *chaopha* was never spoken of by his name. If it was absolutely necessary to name him, the voice was lowered to a whisper as a token of respect.[13] The commoners' houses were never allowed to excel the *chaopha*'s either in height or in design. No one was to ride past his palace, nor were dead bodies, either of men or of animals, carried past it.[14]

---

11 Leach (1954:215–216).
12 Yule (1858:303–305).
13 Milne (1910:108).
14 Scott (1900:408).

Figure 4.1 The front gate of Muang Mao's grand palace. The ancient glory has passed.

In the ideal system, succession to the throne passed from father to son in a direct line. As a rule, the *chaopha*-ship devolved on the eldest son of the *maha devi* (the queen or chief wife). Failing heirs in the direct line, the succession went to the eldest male of the next wife. From reviewing the history of many Tai states in the Shan territory, Pattaya[15] concluded that there appeared to be no rigid rule of succession. In practice, the *chaophas* could name as their successors anyone they wished.[16] If there was no son, or the son was unfit for the throne, the *chaopha*-ship went to a brother or a brother's son. A commoner could also become a *chaopha* by leading a successful rebellion against a tyrant or a weak ruler and getting himself accepted by the people. Collis[17] gave an example of Khun Sang, who was originally a local chief and rose successfully against the then oppressive tyrant and became *chaopha* of Hsenwi in 1885.

---

15 Pattaya (1959:124–125).
16 Woodthorpe (1896:22–23); Cochrane (1915:13–15).
17 Collis (1938:251–253).

Among the Tai of Shan states, a custom of a *chaopha* marrying his half-sister as his queen was mentioned by Yule,[18] so as "to preserve the blood royal".[19] This practice was questioned by Leach,[20] even though it was certainly a fashion of the Burmese court. According to many chronicles of the Tai Daikong,[21] there is no evidence that this practice was customary among the *chaopha* of the Tai states. Some cases of a *chaopha* marrying his half-sister have been reported as having taken place, but these cases are too few and far between to justify the claim that this was a standard practice expected of a ruling *chaopha*.[22]

Normally the *chaopha* had many wives. The principal wife was called *maha devi* whilst his other wives would be appointed as *devi* with priority ranking according to the time of their presentation to the *chaopha*. Having many wives played an important role in the Tai political system since the *devi* of the *chaopha* usually was the daughter of a *chaopha* from another state, the daughter of a minister or from the family of an influential person in the area. Having several wives would enable the *chaopha* to attract persons in various groups as political allies. As influential groups developed ties through marriage with the *chaopha*, the size of the palace and the number of *devis* came to reflect the scope of political power and influence of each *chaopha*. The *chaopha* of large states, for instance the *chaopha* of Muang Seephaw, who died in 1928, had a total of 28 *devis*, whilst the *chaopha* of small townships might have merely two or three *devis*.[23]

The number of *devis* was an important indicator of a *chaopha*'s royal power and greatness, so it was one important factor accounting for the size of the *haw chaopha*, the residence of members of the royal family, the *devis*, relatives and children as well as all the retinue and servants. The *haw chaopha* of Muang Tai was divided into three *haw—haw kham* (golden *haw*), *haw klang* (the middle *haw*) and *haw awn* (the minor *haw*). The *haw kham* or royal palace was the residence of the *chaopha*, the *maha devi* and their children whilst the *haw klang* was usually the residence of his younger brothers or sisters or elder relatives. The *haw awn* was the residence of nephews, nieces, grandchildren or relatives of lower echelons.

---

18 Yule (1858:303).
19 Quoted in Pattaya (1959:130); cf. Milne (1910:78).
20 Leach (1954:216).
21 Nanthasingha (1997).
22 Pattaya (1959:130).
23 Leach (1954:132).

Figure 4.2 A former *devi* of *chaopha* Muang Ti in her royal attire

In practice, the power base of a *chaopha* did not emanate only from the connections or alliances with influential family groups as well as the number of faithful followers, but the important power base of the *chaopha* lay in the control and management of the entire land resources of his territory. The *chaopha* was the one who appointed the *poo heng* (district head) or *poo kay* (village head) who were responsible for the collection of land taxes and delivering them to the *chaopha*. Apart from having to pay taxes, villagers were also expected to provide corvée labour for the *chaopha* such as building and repairing the *haw chaopha*, or certain villages were assigned to carry out specific chores for the *chaopha*: for instance, certain villages were allocated the duties of delivering meat to the *chaopha*, other villages were required to supply vegetables whilst other villages had to look after elephants or horses belonging to the *chaopha*. Villagers were also duty-bound to present gifts to the *chaopha* on various occasions such as birthdays, marriages or funerals.[24] All villagers were also duty-bound to act in defence of their homeland in the event of war.

The *chaopha* had the duty to act as judge in legal cases. In the event that the *poo kay* or *poo heng* made an unjust verdict, the villagers might petition the *chaopha* for a re-trial of the case. The *chaopha* also had to preside or officiate at important religious functions such as at the *poi chong para* ceremony to welcome the return of the Buddha during celebrations marking the end of the lent. Several *chaopha* used revered animals as insignia or totems of the royal family such as the *chaopha* of Muang Mao who had the tiger as the royal family emblem and name, whilst the *chaopha* of Muang Chae Fang had the wasp as insignia.

The *chaopha*'s role was to govern and rule the state according to ancient royal customs assisted by a group of ministers or counsellors with senior monks serving as advisers. The Tai people considered that even the *chaopha* himself did not have the right to defy ancient customs or important Buddhist religious precepts; violations against established traditions could be used as justification leading to the overthrow of the *chaopha* or assassination by political rivals.[25]

Since time immemorial Tai people have held on to the belief that the *chaopha* is a person endowed with utmost righteousness, compassion for the common people as his children and a brave and capable warrior in times of hostilities. Ruling in a manner oppressive to the people, such as excessive taxation, might result in resentment and defiance by refusing to pay taxes followed by massive migration to other states.[26] Migration and showing allegiance to another *chaopha* were a challenge to the legitimate ruling of that *chaopha*. Migration of the masses weakened the productive forces and power of the *chaopha* and could become the starting point of rebellion by people who wanted to overthrow their own leader.

The *chaopha* had an important role to perform as representative of the state in maintaining relationships with other states, so he had to try to build up friendly alliances with the *chaopha* of other states through marriages so as to create bonds of friendship, family association and political relationship as much as possible. A *chaopha* bold and skilful in the martial arts and capable of extending his royal

---

24 T'ien (1986:53).
25 Scott (1900:429).
26 Scott (1900:286).

authority over other states usually sent one of his sons or brothers to become *chaopha* of such states. The *chaopha* of many Tai states were therefore interrelated by blood or through marriage and maintained rapport by frequent regular reunions.[27]

Council of Ministers

The *chaopha* was the head of state, administering and governing the common people by the administrative mechanism of the council of ministers who were advisers to the *chaopha*. The council of ministers comprised from four to twelve persons or more depending on the size of the state or power and influence of the *chaopha* of that state. The council of ministers had duties similar to the cabinet, with meetings to consult on political or civil matters with the *chaopha* every five days. The council of ministers was headed by a royal minister as chairman. The royal minister's office was passed on by descendant line from father to son and the royal minister possessed great power and influence. He looked after the affairs of the state when the *chaopha* happened to be ill, when the *chaopha* was away on journeys to other states, or when the position of *chaopha* was vacant. The entire council of ministers was directly appointed by the *chaopha* under the recommendations of the royal minister. Normally the council of ministers comprised close relatives of the *chaopha* who were appointed as advisers or assigned to look after various departments such as collection of taxes, supervision of the army or adjudication of various lawsuits.

The council of ministers carried out administrative duties in the name of the *chaopha* by assigning responsibilities to district officials to carry out work. Each minister drew no regular salary but acquired a share of land and was able to obtain benefit from the fruits of such land without having to pay taxes. Moreover the ministers received fees from adjudicating lawsuits and also received presents or gifts from merchants and the general public.

---

27 Harvey and Barton (1930:15).

Poo heng and *Poo kay*

The most important leaders at local levels were *poo heng* and *poo kay*; the word "*heng*" in Tai means one thousand. *Poo heng* was the title for the chief of a circle of villages in a certain area, so presumably it may have derived from the ancient tradition that the *poo heng* had the duty to collect tax of one thousand bushels of rice for delivery to the *chaopha* regularly each year. *Poo heng* was the head of a circle of villages directly appointed by the *chaopha*. Generally the *poo heng* came from an influential family and enjoyed respect from the local people. The title of *poo heng* passed on from father to son or to persons in the same family.

The *poo heng*'s important duty was to look after the welfare of the people in his circle of villages, to maintain order, suppress robbers, collect taxes, give decisions on lawsuits when requested and to supervise the work of the *poo kay* or village chief in his territory. The *poo kay* had duties similar to the *poo heng* but at a lesser level—he was chief of a village, responsible for looking after the welfare of the villagers, settling disputes or quarrels and collecting taxes for handing over to the *poo heng*. One of the most important duties of the *poo kay* was to divide paddy land for the people of the village. Tai people considered that all the rice land belonged to the *chaopha*, so a villager had the right of using and occupying paddy land as allocated by the *poo kay* only. When there was an increase of households or new influx of migrants, that village would have to undergo reallocation of working land to suitably accommodate the increased number of households. The *poo kay* was responsible for land allocation in his village. Villagers elected and submitted the name of the *poo kay* to the *chaopha* for appointment. Theoretically, if the majority of villagers were dissatisfied with the performance of the *poo kay* or *poo heng*, the villagers could join forces and send an elder of the village to petition the *amat* (minister) or the *chaopha* to remove the *poo heng* or *poo kay* from office at any time, although such cases scarcely appear on record and this never happened in Lak Chang in the village elders' memory.

Social Classes

Throughout history, Tai society in Daikong consisted of only two classes: the ruling class and the common people. The ruling class included the *chaopha*, royalty and relatives as well as the *amat* (ministers), the majority of the ruling class being related to the *chaopha*.

As the Tai reckon relatives bilaterally and since the *chaopha* normally had several *devi*, the group of relatives or number of persons claiming to be related to the *chaopha* would be rather considerable. Leach[28] suggested that the ruling class in Tai society also included persons who were able to induce servants or the entourage to address them with various titles indicating relationship with the ruling class—such as the word *chao* or *khun*—by claiming affiliation with the *chaopha*. In the ruling class, as the *chaopha* was the centre of relationship and social position, recognition of kinship or lineage on the paternal side was more important than the maternal one.

Tai peasants in general had the right to exploit the land belonging to the *chaopha* according to allocations made by the *poo kay*. The social class of a peasant was lower than that of the ruling class; they engaged in production to feed society whilst the ruling class ruled. The common subjects had to show respect to the ruling class, carry out orders, provide service and pay taxes to the ruling class. The commoners were divided into two groups whose position differed. The first group comprised the majority of Tai Daikong, that is, peasants who engaged in agricultural production, including traders and various artisans. The second group comprised common labourers who, by occupation, engaged in sinful deeds or contravened the Buddhist religious precepts: butchers, fishermen, liquor-dealers and pig-keepers. Tai people are inclined to view this group of people with a lower status than peasants or traders in general. Moreover, members of other ethnic groups such as the Kang or Jingpo are given a status inferior to the ordinary people.

Although Tai society distinctly separated the ruling class from the common people and each class had clearly different rules of conduct, in practice class distinction did not absolutely separate people of each social class. In everyday life, members of the ruling class and ordinary people often crossed the status bar by intermarriage, particularly marriage between a man of the ruling class and the daughter of a villager, a practice which became conventional and commonplace. In the same way, a *devi* or widow of a deceased *chaopha* could remarry a villager, another practice which often took place.[29] Therefore interclass marriage has

---

28 Leach (1954:213–214).
29 Pattaya (1959:142).

become a common practice. However, the interesting factor is that the separation of social classes in Tai society was not an absolute distinction; class was a system of indicating relative position in society. Persons of a lower "class" acknowledged the authority and station of a person of higher status by courteous, respectful manners and behaviour. Villagers in general showed courteous deference towards the *poo kay*, the latter showed courteous deference towards the *poo heng*; the *poo heng* showed courteous deference towards the *amat* (minister) and all the people showed respect and deference towards the *chaopha* in that sequence. The *chaopha* held the highest rank with the uppermost status, removed from all other people. For the general citizen, the *chaopha* appeared all highest, almost godlike, and the *chaopha* had to uphold this social stance by surrounding himself with a royal retinue, residing in a sizeable *haw* and by distancing himself from the ordinary people in general to preserve purity of lineage.

As for the other low-ranking royals who had no ambition to reach the pinnacle of the political ladder, the purity of the royal lineage was probably not something that they had to preserve or be overly concerned with. These royals had closer contact with the common people, their daily lives being intermingled with the people and marriage with ordinary people was a possibility.[30]

Social Groups and Organisations

In the past, important social groups and organisations in a Tai village could be divided into four categories: family group, labour-exchange group, youth group and elders group.

The family group began with blood ties within the family between father, mother and children and extended to relatives of the father's and mother's sides. The family and kin group was the group of people who had closest contact. Family and kinsmen were consulted in every important decision. They were also allies, sources of loans and important labour resources at weddings, funerals and other festivities at various junctions of social life.

The labour-exchange group was the social group extended from the family and kin group to include close neighbours, friends and owners of adjoining paddy

---

30 cf. Collis (1938:134–135).

fields. The labour exchange group would send family members to assist when requested especially in times of hard labour such as rice planting and harvesting to make the work easier and more pleasant. The labour-exchange group was the basis of social contact and mutual assistance on other occasions such as house-building and merit-making activities. Young men and women who were members of the same labour-exchange group had the opportunity of meeting one another while working in the fields or during family celebrations. Occasions conducive to development of intimate contacts between these young men and women were rather plentiful, often leading to love and eventually to marriage. Parents of both sides usually favoured and encouraged marriage between families that enjoyed a close relationship. The marriage would also create closer and stronger ties within the group.

A social group of another type which was very important in Tai society was the youth group. This type of social group was a combination of young men and women of similar age mostly 16–20 years old. This group of youths joined together to form an important force in conducting various affairs in Tai social life.

The youth group in Tai village society began from a grouping of four or five relatives or cousins of similar ages to help out with household chores such as on occasions of marriages or funerals. These young men and women were an important source of labour for preparing places and transporting materials and supplies to enable the occasion to be successfully carried out. Sometimes, the youth group would be formed into an official organisation by combining various youth groups to become an important work force for arranging religious ceremonies of importance such as the village *poi* or merit-making festival.

Normally, young men and women reaching marriageable age would form into a youth group. Becoming a member of the group meant that the social standing of a minor was transformed into that of an adult. The youth group transformed itself into an official social organisation under the supervision of the *poo kay* who appointed leaders from the young men's group and young women's group with the duty to supervise and look after the work of the group. Many villages of large size might break up the youth group into several small teams to compete with each other in carrying out work or to divide their responsibilities. Each team would try to recruit new members from households of affluence and girls who

Figure 4.3 A team of young men and women at a wedding

were pretty, in order to increase the work force and potential of their team. Teams within the youth group would assist in all kinds of work in the village. The young men's group might take on the repairs of temples and carry coffins for burial while the young women's group would make flower arrangements, clean up places, prepare food and wash dishes. Before the time of the Communist revolution, the Tai Daikong favoured celebrating *poi* festivals at each household, each household taking turns to act as host to present gifts to the village temple. Gifts most chosen to be presented to temples were cabinets made of teak primed with black lacquer and covered with gold leaves. These cabinets contained a Buddha image. The young men's group would undertake the task of travelling to the Shan State in Burma to purchase such cabinets and Buddha images to be brought back for presentation to the temples. The youth group was the social organisation responsible for training young men and women in the moral responsibilities, and the roles and duties of an adult. The young men and women would remain members of the group until they married and had a house of their own. Marriage marked the end of their role inside the youth group, with new young men and women coming of age to take their places.

Another social group of great importance in the Tai village society was the elders group comprising men with the highest seniority of each family lineage in the village.

Membership of the elders group normally consisted of about five to eight persons or more. The elders group would be invited to preside at marriage ceremonies, to teach and give advice to the bride and groom and ensure that their marriage conformed with traditions. The elders group also exercised duties when presiding over land partitions and looked after the interests of various households that were members of their kin group. The elders also acted as advisers to the *poo kay* in adjudging various cases within the village. Hence the elders group was an important arm in political society and played a very powerful role in village affairs.

Political Organisations and Social Changes

After the Communist takeover in 1949, the various states in the territories of Daikong or Dehong had their boundaries broken up and then realigned by the Chinese government into five districts (*kang*) namely: Mangshi or Muang Khon, Muang Ti or Liang He, Muang Wan or Long Chuan, Muang La or Ying Jiang, and Muang Mao or Rui Li. In each district a district officer (*poo kang*) was appointed by the Chinese authorities from among the local people to act as official adminstrator, with representatives elected from the populace to sit on the local council, with the duty of supervising the work of the district officer.

The Chinese Communist Party tried to exert influence over the social life of the Tai people by sending officials to conduct affairs and supervise the establishment of official political organisations in four forms: village committee, people's army at village level, women's association and farmers' association. District officers give the people an opportunity to elect the *poo kay*, the election being in a roundabout way: the authorities will make a selection of two or three persons qualified to be *poo kay* and let members of the village cast votes to elect the person they want. In addition, members of the village cast votes to elect another ten persons as the village committee to administer and manage the affairs of the village. The village committee chairman or the *poo kay*, either one of them, will become a member of Communist Party Committee at district level. The Chinese People's Liberation Army sends officers to form the people's army at village level, selecting physically strong young men to undergo training in military duties and tactical warfare for the purpose of maintaining peace within the village and becoming army reserves. The Communist Party also sends officers to form women's groups, holding seminars to enable women to have modern "thoughts" not bound to ancient tradition, to possess leadership and to join more in social activities. The Communist Party arranged to form farmers' groups at village level to propagate Marxist theories, and the ideologies of Chairman Mao as well as important government policies such as collectivisation or new farming techniques.

The Chinese government, in exerting its influence by setting up social organisations at village level, has effected changes in the Tai village society in many respects. The village committee, the majority comprising new members of young men and women, began to have a greater say in decisions relating to the affairs of the village thus causing conflicts with the elders group which originally was the influential group of the village. The values and traditions formerly based on gender, age and seniority as factors in deciding social standing were severely challenged. Conflicts of this nature erupted frequently during the Cultural Revolution.

Samfong gave an account of what happened in Lak Chang village as follows:

> The Red Guard cadres took the village elders and placed them under house arrest in the village school house which was renamed as old people's home and kindergarten and assigning the elders with duties of caring for the children so that their parents can work full-time in the fields.

The establishment of new forms of social organisations also altered traditional norms and social values. Adults and senior persons began to feel increasingly oppressed by these new developments. The formation of the farmers' association and cooperative system to supervise and manage commune farm production also made the household lose control over agricultural production. The Tai farming households began to feel irritated by the cooperatives' meddling and dictating rules concerning management of production in each household. Production problems resulted in increased conflicts when the agricultural products of Lak Chang village were taken away to feed the city population and the quantity of food for the village diminished, as never before.

At the same time, Han Chinese began to migrate and settle in the vicinity of Muang Khon in increasing numbers as never before so that the Tai people began to feel that they had become a minority group. The administration system came under increasing control of the Chinese government. Even though the Tai

Daikong were under the dominance of the Imperial Court for many centuries, the influence of China was limited merely to appointment and recognition of the status of the *chaopha* and the *chaopha* was left alone to govern his own people without interference. For this reason the Tai people have for countless years never felt the domination of China over their political and social way of life. However, after the Communist revolution, the Chinese government tried to exert greater influence by indoctrination and ideological propaganda, including the establishment of social organisations under new systems. The abolition of the *chaopha* system in 1953 caused a great number of Tai people to fall into a state of fearful shock, the changes being no longer bearable. During those years, many villagers fled to the Shan State in Burma in order to escape the new form of oppressive governance. Demolition of the *chaopha* palace, the burning of temples and religious scriptures, the defrocking of monks to become coolies forced to do hard labour, the beatings and murders of the *chaopha* and family members during the Cultural Revolution produced a sense of violent anguish in the minds of the Tai people which transformed into an undercurrent of ethnic tension between the Tai and Han Chinese, resulting in a resurgence and reproduction of the Tai ethnic identity and historical consciousness in the decades to follow.

Even after Deng Xiaoping took control in 1976 and the Chinese government adopted the policy of allowing the people to have greater freedom in agricultural production and trade—abolishing the centralised farming system, communes as well as social organisations that the government had set up in the villages—still the feelings of conflict and scars of wounds deeply inflicted on the minds of the Tai people remained clearly visible. The Tai people still felt that the Chinese government or the *khay* (Han Chinese) people had interfered too much with their own lives and began to express resentment towards the *khay* people in various forms and manners.

In Lak Chang village, the antipathetic feelings towards the *khay* people are expressed by various means. For instance, the Tai peasants choose not to sell newly harvested rice to *khay* merchants and prefer to sell only the surplus or *left-over* rice from the previous agricultural year. Endogamous marriage has now become a standard practice. Some Lak Chang villagers explicitly forbid their children to marry different ethnic groups. More importantly, during the past two decades, the demands for local agricultural products have increased rapidly and the value of paddy land has also increased. Land-use patterns have become more intensified and ethnic tensions between the Tai and the Han Chinese over landholdings have also increased.

During the late 1980s, a group of five *khay* families migrated to settle in Lak Chang village by purchasing land within the village from a few Tai families and building houses at the entrance to the village.[31] In 1994, due to an increase in Tai farmer households, the land committee and the village elders convened a meeting for a new allocation of the village farmland to suit the changing needs and reality. The meeting consisted of the *poo kay*, members of the land committee, the elders group and officials of the district acting as witnesses. All five *khay* households presented demands to the land committee for a share of farmland by arguing that they were now part of the village. The demands made by the *khay* newcomers were met by fierce opposition from the village land committee and the elders group.

Yee, who chaired the land committee of the village at that time, gave an account thus: "The land committee refused to let the *khay* people have a parcel of land because their fathers had never contributed their labour to open up farmland in Lak Chang village." The reasons of the village committee were that the *khay* people were not real members of the village and the forefathers or ancestors of these people had had no part in developing the place nor had they earned a living on the village land before. These people therefore had no right to the use of the village land like other offspring of Lak Chang villagers who have a right as direct descendants.

The district officers who were *khay* people argued that these people had a legal right because, according to domicile registration, they were lawfully living in Lak Chang village and all were citizens of China. However, the *poo kay*, the land committee and elders of the village invariably refused the *khay* householders rights over the village farmland of the kind proposed by the officers. Even though the officers threatened to bring the matter up with the district office, to consider removal of this land committee, as well as to relieve the *poo khay* of his position, the people of Lak Chang still adhered to their original resolution. Meetings to resolve this problem were held five times but to no avail until the rice-planting

---

31 In Daikong, household land within the village can be bought and sold freely but farm land is state property and therefore cannot be bought or sold.

season approached and the matter still could not be settled, resulting in the process of land allocations coming to a halt, with other Tai farming households who had not received land allocations before suffering from this problem as well.

After vehement arguments for a period of several days, the land committee issued a resolution that the village meeting allocate farmland to the five *khay* households of an area merely one-third of the land that a Tai household receives, that is, each *khay* household was to receive farmland of three *mou*. All the *khay* householders protested against this ruling but the land committee affirmed their decision saying, "We give only this, take it or leave it."

Although the people of Lak Chang were fearful of the powers of the district officer and the representatives of the Chinese authorities, a feeling deeply inflicted following the Communist revolution, the villagers were united in opposition— "concerning farmland, we cannot give in"—and in the end the *khay* householders conceded to the decision of the land committee and accepted the said quantity of land. From that time on, the people of Lak Chang issued a village law absolutely forbidding any villager to sell household land to an outsider to prevent a recurrence of this problem in the future.

Conflicts, as in the case of farmland allocation, may be one instance showing that the Tai, as a minority under the influence of China for a long time, although accepting authoritative rule and accepting Chinese culture and traditions in many ways as their own and unavoidably acknowledging themselves as a part of China, have not remained passive receptors of government policies. They have, however, tried to struggle for the rights of self-determination, as well as engage in the struggle to define a meaningful identity of Tai-ness which is deeply rooted in farming community, land, rice, Buddhism and other cultural symbols. We shall return to discuss this matter in detail again in the final chapter.

Chapter Five

RELIGIOUS BELIEFS AND RITUALS

The religious beliefs of the Tai Daikong are based on the Buddhist religion of the Theravadha sect which spread to the Tai Daikong people via Burma and the Tai people in Shan State. Even though the Buddhist religion originated in India 2,500 years ago, traces of the Buddhist religion began to emerge for the first time in Burma during the fifth century AD.[1] Legends of the Tai people in Shan State and the Tai Daikong spoke of the Tai ancestors as professing the Buddhist faith during the sixth century AD.[2]

Buddhist beliefs and rituals played an important role in the lifestyle and viewpoints of the Tai to the extent that some scholars are of the opinion that being Tai and belief in Buddhism are identical.[3] Buddhism is deeply embedded in culture, art, music, architecture, articles of faith and mentality of the Tai Daikong and has also played an important role in the social and cultural life of the Tai up to the present. The Buddhist religion was severely persecuted during the period of the Cultural Revolution, with temples being torched, stupas demolished, monks and novices caught and defrocked, the Tripitaka and Buddhist religious scripts burnt, yet from the early 1980s onwards the temples and various religious edifices in Daikong area—including the temple in Lak Chang village—were gradually repaired and restored, or newly built.

---

1 Coedes (1968:17–18).
2 Nanthasingha (1997).
3 Leach (1954).

105

From a cultural perspective, it would not be an overstatement if we were to say that almost all aspects of the Tai culture have derived from Buddhist beliefs. Important rituals including merit-making or charitable ceremonies and beliefs connected with production and daily living are almost entirely entwined with Buddhism. The Jataka stories of the various incarnations of the Buddha before enlightenment became important themes of legends and folktales of the Tai Daikong. Architectural styles such as temples and pagodas, including ethnic symbols such as the peacock and the long drum, are a blend of Burmese and Tai religious traditions. Tai Daikong dramatics such as the famous bird dance are also influenced by traditional celebrations welcoming the return of the Buddha to earth according to the Tai belief. Calculation methods relating to the world and universe, relationships between human beings and surrounding conditions, relationships between human beings themselves and between human beings and other supernatural things are mostly based on Buddhist beliefs.

Buddhism also plays an important role in the social life of the village. The importance of Buddhism in the lives of the Tai can be measured from the time, resources and energy contributed wholeheartedly to the Buddhist religion and various merit-making or charitable ceremonies. Buddhist teachings also dominate the conduct of the Tai from birth through adult life. In old age a Tai favours visiting temples, observing the precepts, practising meditation and using the greater part of leisure hours in religious pursuits.

Buddhism is of greatest significance to the Tai identity in village society. The predominant element of being a Tai is to be a Buddhist. The Tai separate themselves from surrounding ethnic groups such as the Han, Jingpo and Lisu for one important reason—these people are not Buddhists. For this reason being a Tai means and includes unconditionally being a Buddhist. Persons who are not of the Buddhist faith are viewed as outsiders and are excluded from the Tai village community.

Buddhism also plays an important role in defining social norms and proper behaviour. Goodness and being a good person are judged by the standard of observing Buddhist religious precepts, so persons occupied in slaughtering animals or distilling liquor for sale afford a rather inferior status in Tai society. In the same way, persons who regularly breach the five precepts, who are in the habit of taking lives, drinking or committing adultery, are treated as social outcasts by villagers. The influence played by Buddhism in the daily lives of the Tai people can also be seen in the inclination of villagers to chat about merit-making as well as the teaching of Buddhism on various occasions. Old people are fond of entertaining children by reciting Jataka tales and stories relating to the Buddha.

Although the Tai people stress the importance of Buddhism in their daily lives, in fact the religion and religious beliefs of the Tai Daikong, like other societies, are interwoven with various forms of beliefs, in particular belief in spirits, black magic, incantations and witchcraft. These beliefs are deeply rooted in and are inseparable from the religious faith of the Tai. For this reason, some scholars are of the opinion that Tai people believe in Buddhism but they are unable to weed out the spurious elements that adulterate their Buddhist faith.[4] Although the Tai people are well aware that Buddhism and animism are theoretically separated, in practice these beliefs are closely intertwined in ritual and daily life. For example, Lah, Sam Fong's youngest daughter-in-law, married and lived with her husband for quite a number of years but had no children. She was urged by the elders to visit the temple frequently to make merit and give alms generously so that the couple's meritorious acts would bless them with a child. At the same time, Lah's grandmother taught her to make small clay dolls, dressed up in pretty clothing, to be hung up near a Buddha statue in the temple with the belief that the spirit that will lead the child's soul to be born, will acknowledge her heart's desire and help her to soon have a child.

Buddhism and Animism in Daily Life

Buddhist beliefs and practices in the daily life of the Tai people were heavily influenced by Burmese traditions. King Anoratha of Burma was converted to Buddhism in 1058 AD and played an important role in spreading Buddhism rapidly throughout the various parts of Burma. When Bahyinnong completely subdued the various townships of the Tai people in Shan State in 1562 AD, the Tai people in Shan State began to convert to the Buddhist religion of the Theravaddha sect. The influence of Theravaddha Buddhism spread from Shan State to the Daikong area later on.[5]

---

4 Cochrane (1915).
5 Scott (1900:334–336); Milne (1910:25–29); Cochrane (1915:317–326).

Buddhist beliefs derive from Dharma tenets in the Tripitaka which the Tai Daikong received from Burma. The Tripitaka, which was in the Pali language, restricted studies in the Dharma principles only to a small number of monks who were able to read Pali. During the Cultural Revolution some of these monks were caught and disrobed whilst some escaped to Burma, resulting in disruption of the Buddhist religion for a lengthy period up to the present time. The beliefs—including understanding of the Buddhist Dharma principles—of the Tai Daikong, therefore derive mostly from reading annals and folklore written in the Tai language adapted from the Jataka stories with insertions of Dharma principles of the Buddhist religion, rather than from direct studies of the Tripitaka script.

The Tai Daikong believe in reincarnation of all forms of life according to the law of karma determined by one's past deeds. The condition and fate of each person are the result of good and bad deeds accumulated during previous existences. The Tai therefore favour making merit, giving alms, observing religious precepts and doing work for the temples in order to accumulate merit which one would depend upon in the next life. Accumulation of merit will ensure that a person will be born in a better position until accumulation of virtue is great enough for them to reach Nirvana.

It may be this reason that makes Tai forsake worldly matters and turn towards religion from the time they reach middle age. It is the normal custom that when a women passes 40 years of age, she will change her clothes from pretty bright colours to a skirt and blouse of dark colour and begin to attend religious rituals more often. A Tai will give alms to the temple, present Buddhist statues, build pagodas and donate money and labour for repairing temples. These works are considered acts of high merit because they are for the preservation of the Buddhist religion. Conversely, breaches of the precepts, especially the slaughter of animals and taking life, are considered as hideous deeds or very sinful acts which a Tai tries painstakingly to avoid.

Almost every village in Daikong has its temple. Some temples which were destroyed during the Cultural Revolution have begun to be repaired or built anew. However, a scarcity of monks is being experienced in Daikong as the values of entering monkhood begin to change. Formerly, parents sent their children, particularly their sons, to learn the letters in the temple. Monks are the teachers of Tai and Pali languages as well as moral ethics to the children of the village. Every male must take the vows of monkhood for at least one Lent before marrying and having a family in order to undergo spiritual training to be ready for life's responsibilities. However, in the last three decades, schools and teachers have begun to take over the roles of the temples and monks. Religious opposition and continuous Communist ideological propaganda, as well as smaller families due to the rigorous birth-control policy augmented by labour requirements for year-round agricultural production, may have been the cause for the decline in ordinations into monkhood.

Nevertheless, the faith in Buddhism remains incredibly strong. Elderly people like to take their children to the temples to hear sermons or simply to chat with monks, sweep the temple grounds, clean up dust and arrange flowers for worship. Villagers will stop working on Buddhist holidays to go to the temple to listen to religious sermons. Normally, Tai monks will not go out to receive morning food offerings like the monks in Thailand do. Each household will take turns to present food to the monks regularly on a daily basis. Temples also serve as the centre for merit-making rituals and religious festivities for the entire village.

From the Tai's point of view, beliefs other than teachings of the Buddhist religion are collectively said to be matters concerning animism and magic which include occultism, incantations, tattoos, geomancy, shamanism and healing. Animistic beliefs and practices are closely intertwined with Buddhist religious beliefs so that they contain no contradictions. A Tai believes that every living being and material thing possesses a soul which is a more refined essence of matter. These souls have the power to control the growth and development of all such things. They may become endowed with individual conscious life and, when freed from their grosser elements, they become beings that preside over the various departments of nature. Some wander at will through space and can transform themselves with great versatility; others, more pure and ethereal, rise to the regions of the stars. Hence, stars and planets are not worldly but divinities, and their motions control the destinies of man.[6] In the ancient Tai myth of Genesis it is said that all spirits as well as the earth and the universe were created by Indra who miraculously caused some primeval eggs, which already existed without his action, to be fertilised and hatched into gods of various kinds: the sun-gods, the moon-gods, the gods of all natural forces—of light and air, of wind and sky, of forests and

---

6 Pattaya (1959:291).

streams, of spirits, of men and even of dreams.[7] When human beings die, their souls will be born again without end. Bad people when they die have to repay for all their misdeeds before they can be born again.

The Tai believe that the soul or spirit is of the same basic nature as things that live—they have goodness and badness, strength and weakness, are benevolent or malevolent. For this reason man does not have to be under the control of the spirits all the time but he can bargain with the spirits by various means, such as propitiations, enticements or threats (by incantations) in the same manner as one person does with another. Evil spirits are to be feared because they interfere with a person's life, cause illness and disease, accidents or bad luck on various occasions. These are the evil spirits that villagers come into contact with during their daily lives. The customary practice of the Tai is to propitiate spirits and this is not confined only to benevolent spirits. Often the villagers propitiate evil spirits by way of offering bribes or asking them to hold the peace and not hurt their households. Appeasing the spirits like this is usually done at times of trouble or sickness, or to prevent various calamities during house-building or when long journeys are to be made.[8]

The Tai Daikong separate the benevolent spirits absolutely from the malevolent ones. The good spirits do good to people by giving protection, guarding people, households, trees and crops in the fields as well as the well-being of the villagers, whilst the evil spirits are purposely mischievous and malevolent. Normally, evil spirits are more powerful than good spirits but the powers of both types of spirits also lie within the laws of karma. Good spirits cannot save a person when his time is up; likewise bad spirits cannot do harm to a virtuous person. For this very reason, to propitiate, bribe or entice evil spirits to stop attacking a sick person may not be successful—the patient may die, the bad luck or disasters may persist—due to the result of past life deeds that give the evil spirits the chance to exercise greater ruthless power and punish this unfortunate person. Therefore the powers of spirits are restricted by the merits of virtue or by karma as destined by deeds that one has accumulated in past life. Thus Buddhist and animistic beliefs are reconciled.

The vital reasons for a spirit to harm a person may be because that person has offended the spirit or may be due to certain acts performed at an inappropriate

---

7 Cochrane (1915:116–118).
8 Milne (1910:122).

time, or it may be that the influence of their horoscope has destined that they shall encounter misfortune during that time frame, or it may be due to the maliciousness of that spirit itself.[9]

From ancient times every Tai household usually has had a spirit house installed in the compound to be the dwelling place of the guardian spirit whose duty is to give protection to members of that household. At present the erection of guardian spirit houses has been neglected. In Lak Chang, there does not appear to be even a single spirit house remaining in any of the households. There is only one "*chao baan*" spirit tower serving as protector of the village. According to the belief of the Tai Daikong, the *chao baan* represents the soul of the first ancestor to die since the building of the village. The *chao baan* spirit of Lak Chang is that of a woman named Yod Saeng. According to customary practice at times of various rituals—such as marriages, funerals, when sickness occurs, before planting or harvesting rice—the villagers will bring vegetarian food and fruit as offerings to the *chao baan* to ask for protection. The *chao baan* spirit will be able to protect the villagers only in the household area. When leaving the village, Tais in the past favour propitiating spirits that guard rivers and streams, mountains and forests for help according to particular needs.

If a member of the household becomes ill and cannot be cured or if an illness recurs time and again, the villager will go to a medium to ask for help in finding the cause of illness. The medium in Lak Chang, an old man nearly 80 years of age, will interrogate the sick person regarding his actions to find out what he had done to incur the wrath of the demon who thus punished him. What causes the spirit to attack may be some action on the part of the person which has offended the spirit, or some action that has been performed at an inauspicious moment, which exposes the person to the spirit's attack; or it may be because of the inherent malevolent nature of the spirit itself. Thereafter, the medium will disclose the method of dispelling the bad luck such as to make offerings to beg forgiveness and to stop inflicting punishment. The villager may erect a small shrine in the compound, near a bridge or under a tree, to propitiate the demon so that it will stop hurting the member of his household.[10]

When Saeng, the youngest son of Sam Fong, became sick for many days for no reason, Sam Fong visited the medium and asked him to find out which evil spirit

9 Milne (1910:109–110).
10 Thorp (1945:136); Pattaya (1959:293).

111

had maliciously made his son sick. Saeng had nightmares due to the fever and was not conscious, so the medium was unable to question him regarding his actions. The medium therefore went into a trance to ask the demon and found that Saeng was being molested by the *phee kho* (water spirit) because he had failed to make offerings to the water spirit before planting rice, thus making the *phee kho* angry. Sam Fong therefore performed the rites of begging the *phee kho* for forgiveness by erecting a small shrine near the bridge crossing the main sluice at the end of the village, according to the advice of the medium, bringing pork, rice, white wine and flowers. Sam Fong said that on the next morning Saeng's feverish condition disappeared miraculously.

Newborn infants, women just after childbirth and sick persons in convalescence are especially susceptible to being maligned by evil spirits and have to be protected by charms and talismans such as large needles attached on the headband or scarf of newborn infants or the wrist-tying of strings duly blessed by a person with mystical incantations.

Present-day Tai Daikong people still maintain beliefs regarding geomancy, particularly matters concerning building of houses and constructing burial grounds of ancestors. When constructing a house or burial place, a knowledgeable astrologer must be invited to choose its direction and location to ensure that such constructions are auspicious and conducive to the well-being of its occupants in the future.[11] A Tai believes in matters of auspicious moments, when fixing the appropriate time for building homes, for burials and other important ceremonies. For this reason, almost every Tai village has an astrologer to determine the time to ensure auspices. Tais also have many taboos regarding time, such as cutting fingernails or toenails on days coinciding with the day of one's birth; for instance, a person born on Monday may cut nails on any day except Monday. Tais are also in favour of charms and talismans to guard against evil spirits or to attract feelings of kindliness and friendliness, including the tattooing of mystic writings with the belief that they will be invulnerable and no dangers whatever can approach them.

The belief system of the Tai Daikong, whether they are Buddhist religious beliefs or beliefs in spirits, play an important part in the daily conduct and life of the Tai, including social relationships at the village level. Participation in rituals, merit-making and religious festivities play important roles in augmenting good

---

11 Milne (1910:183); Cochrane (1915:137).

relationships between families, friends and neighbours. Invitations to ceremonies are occasions for making-merit and reaffirming the bonds of social relations.

The belief in merit plays an important part in establishing social order as well as status and prestige of various households in the village. Arranging ceremonies for making-merit or *poi* (festivals), including marriage and funeral ceremonies on a grand scale, bestows honour, prestige and social status upon the host. In social terms, to make merit means showing that a person possesses virtue by holding parties, giving alms, building pagodas and temples. All these things are tangible aspects of virtuous august grandeur heaping higher social prestige and status upon the donor and respect for his greater merit.

Beliefs and Rituals in Tai Society

Rituals are social displays that support and confirm religious beliefs. Rituals help man to have confidence in life, to adjust himself to changes according to age and to face various crises that may take place. In anthropology,[12] we can distinguish three types of ritual action: expressive, instrumental and commemorative. Expressive ritual serves as a vehicle for manifesting emotions, attitudes and sentiments felt toward the religious sacra. It plays a part in expressing collective disposition, reaffirming piety in religious principles and beliefs or a showing of respect for things sacred. In Daikong, for instance, the Buddha, the Dhamma (Buddhist teaching and precepts) and the Sangha (Buddhist monks) are objects of intense reverence, and the performance of many Buddhist rituals is a means of expressing veneration, homage and devotion to these representations. Instrumental ritual, performed to achieve some purposive end, is rather more complicated. The end may be some extrinsic goal—physical (health, beauty), social (wealth, power, fame) or natural (plentiful harvest, rainfall)—which could be attained either in the present life or not until after death. Sometimes, however, the end to be achieved by instrumental ritual is an intrinsic goal, that is, a spiritual, emotional or meditative change in the self. Commemorative ritual is performed in remembrance or celebration of some event, historical or mythological, sacred in the annals of the religious tradition. In Daikong, for

---

12 Spiro (1982:191–192).

instance, many rituals serve to commemorate an event in the life of the Buddha, such as commencement of Lent, Makhabuja or Visakhabuja. The majority of Buddhist religious rituals are in this category.

In addition, we can also divide rituals that are performed periodically into three types. The first type are calendrical rituals. They are cyclical, performed on predictable occasions, at fixed periods and periodic intervals. The second type are life-cycle rituals. They are related to birth, initiation, marriage and death. The third type is the crisis ritual. They are performed to extricate the actor from a calamity which she is presently suffering or to save her from one which is or may be impending.

Annual Rituals and Celebrations in Daikong

Religious rituals of the Tai Dikong are mostly connected with timetables based on the lunar calendar. Such rituals are chronologically arranged, that is, they are held regularly at fixed time periods.

New Year festivals. Tais commence the cycle of religious rituals with celebrations of the New Year in the month of April which coincides with the Thai Songkran festivals. Children and persons of lower status will pour water on the hands of elders and playfully splash one another with water, similar to Thai customs and pleasantries. The New Year festivals are times for enjoyment, flirtations between young men and maidens, feasts and gambling within the village. The old and elderly will celebrate the New Year by visiting temples to make merit or they may observe the precepts throughout the festival, so as to commence the year with an accumulation of merit.

At present, the Tai New Year festive season has caught on with the Han Chinese and other ethnic groups. In Muang Khon the New Year celebrations of the Tai are held on a grand scale, with traditional Tai dancing and playful water splashing on roadways throughout the three-day period.

Visakhabuja day. The Tai observe the day of the full moon in the month of May as the occasion to celebrate the Buddha's birthday, enlightenment and attainment of complete bliss. The Tai treat Visakhabuja as the time for making-merit, cleaning and repairing the village temple, with the custom of watering the Bo tree, which is the emblem of the Buddhist religion. Watering the Bo tree signifies the dedication of oneself to the support and continuity of the religion. At present, Visakhabuja is not so vigorously celebrated as in former days, as this period is the time that the majority of villagers are fully engaged in agricultural production with overwhelming chores that leave very little time for arranging celebrations during this period.

Kao phansa: The three-month period from the full moon of July through to the full moon of October may be called the Buddhist lent. Monks or *chao chong* may not travel for that period and it is also a solemn season for laymen as well. Marriages cannot be performed, plays and other forms of public entertainment are forbidden and devout Buddhists attempt to observe the *wan pra* (Buddhist sabbath) as frequently as possible during this time. Villagers will visit the temple to make merit and listen to sermons every holiday throughout the period. On *ok phansa* day (end of lent), the Tai Daikong in almost every village will arrange merit-making activities on a grand scale called *poi chong* or "celebrations for the lord". According to ancient concept or belief, the Tai Daikong pass on the story that the Lord Buddha went up to the second level of heaven to preach a sermon for his mother, and on his return to earth the Tai people therefore built a palace made of bamboo, decorated with cloth of beautiful colours and arranged group dancing to greet his return. During the *ok phansa* or *chong* celebrations, the villagers will beautifully decorate temples in the village and hold parties by inviting friends from other villages to join in the merriment.

Tod kathin (presentation of robes): From the end of October onwards, the Tais favour the custom of *tod kathin* in the belief that persons who perform the *kathin* ceremony—presenting the robes and various useful articles to monks—will live happily and become wealthy. Following the harvest season, from October until March, Tai people prefer to arrange *poi* celebrations or merit-making celebrations of the village including marriages and other auspicious celebrations.

Poi festivals: Prior to the Cultural Revolution, the *poi*[15] were the most grand and jubilant of all celebrations in the Tai farming villages. After the harvest season has ended, news of *poi* celebrations spreads all over the village and its vicinity. Some households in the village are prepared to host the *poi* celebrations. One household may dedicate itself to donating a Buddha statue to the temple, another household

---

15 Tien (1986:12–35).

Figure 5.1 A poi festival in Muang Khon

may make dedication by donating a cabinet for holding the Tripitaka, whilst yet another may host the *kathin* offerings by specifying a sum of money. The host of a *poi* celebration may consist of only one household or may include other households of close relatives or friends.

After the various households have dedicated themselves to act as hosts of the *poi* festivals and have fixed the days with the temple in order, the news of the festivals spreads throughout the village as well as around the surrounding villages. News regarding a *poi* festival affects the village people in at least two ways. In one way, the householders who dedicated themselves to host the *poi* festivals begin to hear that a lot of people are excited and happy over the *poi* festival on this occasion. The host begins to worry that the number of guests attending the festival may exceed the ability of the host to offer them a good reception. The large number of guests attending the festival means that the expenses will increase correspondingly. On the other hand, households that hold a position of affluence but did not intend to host this *poi* festival at first, now begin to catch on with excitement to the news and may think back on the honours and high regard they had received from the community when hosting the festival last time to the point of wanting to join in as host of this festival. A father and his children, brothers and sisters may make a collection to act as host of festivals. Some households borrow money from close relatives and friends to pay the expense of hosting such festivals.

It would be rather difficult for outsiders, especially for persons who had never attended a Tai *poi* festival, to understand the feelings of the villagers towards having a *poi* festival. The importance of *poi* festivals in the life of a Tai can be put at least at two levels. At the first level, they are accumulations of merits as the Tai believe that the host of a *poi* festival, including his descendants, will go to heaven after death. Arranging for a *poi* festival therefore is like buying insurance or building up merit for enjoying happiness in the next world. At the social level, a *poi* festival helps the host to become a person of esteem, gaining honour and respect from members of the village, enjoying an enhanced social standing and status. A household that often arranges *poi* festivals increases its social standing and status. In real life, households that are affluent enough to arrange *poi* festivals, may host *poi* festivals again and again without becoming weary of it. When a *poi* festival is being held, every activity in the village will come close to a complete standstill for weeks on end. Everyone in the village will await in anticipation the *poi* festival. In a large village, which may have several hundred households, it would be difficult for a host consisting of only one single household to be able to entertain all the villagers, not to mention guests from other villages who come to join the party without invitation. Should the host drive away guests who are not of his village or is unable to accord them a befitting welcome, he would lose face. For this reason, a host would be happy if other households offer to become joint hosts.

The various households that decide to act as joint hosts will send representatives to negotiate the agreement and discuss various matters, such as fixing the date of the festival, the journey to obtain the Buddha images, priestly offerings and other things for presentation to the temple at the *poi* festival. The households acting as host will send household members to travel together with a group of young villagers for the purpose of buying Buddha images and other things from Nam Kham village on the Burma side of the border, setting the time for the group of young men to travel back a little before the date of the festival. Joint purchases in large quantities enable the host to save a considerable amount of money for the cost of the goods and expenses for the trips. The *chao chong* or monk of the village by implication becomes the adviser to the sponsor committee, giver of opinion relating to the size and shape of the Buddha image that the temple wants, as well as suggestions regarding prices and types of other paraphernalia.

When the day fixed for the trip comes, every household of the sponsors will send its representatives to travel with the group of young villagers to Nam Kham. The sponsors have to engage scores of village young men to help in carrying back the

Buddha image and other valuable items. The trip from Muang Khon to Nam Kham takes four days each way. Trips of this nature are heavy work because, apart from having to shoulder the Buddha image as well as other goods, the journey has to be undertaken with care to prevent damage occurring and the travelling party has to camp in the forests in a cold, damp atmosphere risking the dangers of jungle fever and ambush by *khang* marauders. The meagre fees earned by the young men from the sponsors are poor compensation for the hardship and dangers of many days' travel and camping. However, members of the youth group still take on such journeys regularly to bring back Buddha images because, according to the Tai belief, those taking part in such journeys obtain grace and merit second only to the sponsors of the *poi* festivals.

On the way back, one day before reaching the village, the group of youths will send a representative to inform the households of the sponsors to make preparations. The sponsors begin to feel uneasy with countless worries as to whether or not the Buddha image brought back will be beautiful or whether the various things have suffered damage during the journey. When the group of young men and the party reach the house, they will receive a warm welcome. The sponsors' households will go and wait at the entrance of the village to receive them with gong and long drum beatings leading the procession to welcome the Buddha image to the sponsors' house. The weariness from many days' long journey disappears almost entirely. The sponsors of the *poi* festival will offer the utmost welcome to the group of young men and the party. All will sit down to enjoy the food and drinks together from the afternoon until late at night. Various exciting incidents that took place during the journey will be narrated with merriment. Householders of the sponsors and the group of young men that travelled to bring the Buddha image often cultivate friendships that in future develop into firm and steadfast ties.

When the Buddha image and other merit-making items arrive at the village, the householders of each sponsor will take them to the temple. The sponsors will invite close friends and relatives to help in the task by solemnly parading the Buddha image from the village to the temple. The monks will chant prayers of felicitations and blessings on the sponsors' households. After every one of the sponsors' households has presented all the items to the temple, then the important day that all await is due. The entire village begins to stir with lively activity. All of the sponsors' household including various relatives will be busy arranging for the party, preparing food and wine to entertain guests joining the *poi* celebrations. The old people and women engage in sewing handsome robes for the Buddha image, sewing curtains, tablecloths for the offering tables, temple floor-covering material, suits of yellow robes for the monks; hanging banners or flags for decorating the temple; and preparing other paraphernalia to be presented to the temple and monks.

The sponsors' household members have been preparing tables for entertaining relatives and friends for weeks in advance. Friends and relatives from other villages in numbers make social calls and mill about as spectators. The sponsors from all households will start sending representatives to welcome the guests, friends and relatives who have joined the *poi* festival to congratulate the sponsors on the appointed day. Visitors joining the festival usually bring rice, woven cloth and meat with them to present to the sponsors as gifts for the occasion.

On the *poi* festival day, all the households of the sponsors transform themselves into a village meeting point and entertainment centre. Within the household compound, scores of tables are set with food to entertain visiting guests for three consecutive days and nights. Guests drink and dine in continuous feasting, the sponsors' households having to recruit friends and relatives to prepare victuals, set tables, serve food, wash dishes and plates as well as other chores lasting throughout the festival time.

At dawn of the first festival day, a group of young men will parade through the village, beating gongs, long drums and playing music creating a euphoric atmosphere for the whole village. Guests from within and outside the village, dressed in their newest and finest suits, will proceed to the donors' houses with smiling faces to offer congratulations to the donors for their benevolent acts and merits acquired. The unhurried and gentle manners of the guests appear to completely reverse those of the donors' household members who scurry about to prepare food and beverages. The guests, relatives and friends are invited to take seats and partake of the first meal of the *poi* festival. After the morning meal, the host will perform the rite of "receiving the lord", that is, receiving the Buddha image back to the house.

The host and all the villagers will assemble outside the house and arrange a procession to the temple to take the Buddha image back home temporarily to allow the guests a chance of joyful admiration. Household members of each donor will gather all the items intended for presentation to the temple and the monks—such as Buddha statues, the cabinet for holding the Tripitaka, the robes, blankets, sandals, thermos flasks, lamps, bedding, tea pots, dishes and curtains—and display them on the verandah for all the visitors to view.

Throughout the three days of the festival, visiting guests who drop in to drink and dine will praise the beauty of the Buddha image, the magnanimity of the sponsor and give blessings that he may become richer and richer.

The next day, the second day of the *poi* festival, is regarded as the most important day. The sponsor will install a set of tables for worshipping the Buddha image so that guests who come to visit can worship the Buddha. The elder of the household will sit on a chair beside the Buddha image. When guests participating in the festival walk up to worship the Buddha image and pay respects to the elder of the household, this gesture signifies that the elder or head of the host's household is the one who is given the highest honour and respect by every guest and visitor who attends the festival.

In former times, the sponsor of the *poi* festival would invite the *chaopha* to attend on the second day. The *chaopha* might travel there himself or send a representative to congratulate the sponsor for this merit-making festival. The holding of a *poi* festival therefore was the occasion when the villagers might talk with or receive the *chaopha* or his representative. On the other hand, in attending a *poi* festival, the *chaopha* was able to become aware of the welfare and problems of the people under his control.

On the afternoon of the third day, the sponsor will arrange a huge procession led by a large group of musicians with drums, gongs and pipes playing lively tunes. Following the musicians will be a troupe of maidens each wearing beautiful dresses and adornments, followed by a group of youths shouldering a bamboo palanquin bearing the Buddha image and various presents to the village temple. The villagers will pack both sides of the road to have a view and will follow the procession to the temple.

The sponsors and family members wearing brand-new dresses lead the Buddha image with the procession. In sponsoring a *poi* festival, the sponsor and his household must toil hard for many years, saving bit by bit to accumulate money for the cost of a festival. The duration of the *poi* festival is a special occasion when the sponsor becomes the admiration of everyone on all sides for three whole days. When the procession reaches the temple and has completed three circular rounds, the sponsor leads the Buddha image and various offerings into the temple for official presentation to the monk. Thereafter all the villagers will join in chanting prayers. The monk will give a sermon with felicitations and blessings to the sponsors and families to enjoy lasting peaceful happiness.

On completion of the rituals, each donor family will bring a bamboo pole about 10 metres high and erect it in front of the temple, one pole for each family, with a banner or flag attached to the top of the pole whilst the bottom part is decorated with banana plants. Trays of food and fruit will be tied to the bottom part of the pole to propitiate spirits. *Toongs* (flag) of the Tai Daikong are similar in shape to the *toongs* of the northern Thai people. The majority are made of woven cloth some 15–20 centimetres wide and about two to three metres long embroidered with beautiful designs. The designs favoured by the Tai people for *poi* festivals are mostly of pagodas or seven-tiered umbrellas, embroidered with brightly coloured thread on white cloth. The Tai people tell the story that, during the time of the Buddha, a widow heard the news that the Lord Buddha would be passing through her village. Her neighbours all prepared trays of good food together with the finest robes to be presented to the Lord Buddha. This old widow had only a little money and she took all of it to buy thread and was able to obtain merely two rolls which she could weave into only one long strip of cloth. When the Buddha arrived, this old woman presented this piece of cloth to him. The people who attended the Buddha all laughed in contempt of her gift of so little worth. The Buddha accepted the cloth from the widow and gave a lesson saying: "This strip of cloth was a gift of countless value because it was a gift that came with utmost piety." From that time on the *toong* became the symbol of benefaction and merit-making with utmost piety in commemoration of that widow.

When the *poi* festival comes to an end, the sponsor is likely to hang a *toong* some place in front of the temple as a symbol. The Tai people believe that when the sponsor of a *poi* dies, he will go to heaven; his ancestors and his descendants will also obtain grace from the merit-making and will likewise go to heaven. The *toongs* of *poi* festivals are therefore the symbols of reservations made in heaven for the donor and members of his family.

Poi festivals of the Tai Daikong, apart from being an important occasion for celebration after finishing hard work in the fields and farms, renew the good relations between kin groups and members of the whole village who are usually invited to join the festival, as well as being an occasion for making-merit and creating esteem for the donor. *Poi* festivals also play an important part in providing training to a new generation of youths to start learning about their duties and responsibilities to society. The youth group plays the important role of acting as representatives of the donor in taking the journey to bring back Buddha statues as well as in purchasing the various articles for presentation to the temple, not to mention being the basic labour force for making preparations and repairs to the temple prior to holding the *poi* festival. The group of maidens has the basic role of assisting elders in tidying up and beautifying the temple as well as assisting the donor with all sorts of handicraft work.

Presently, *poi* festivals, in which various households in the village join as donors in the above manner, have declined because the increase in agricultural production has saddled every person in the village with greater duties on the farms and trading their products than in former times. Nowadays, the Tai Daikong favour arranging *poi* festivals or merit-making events at temples as activities for which everyone in the village acts as joint donors, with the group of elders of the village acting as the committee for such events. *Poi chong* therefore is of a nature similar to *poi* festivals of old in almost every respect. The difference lies only in the fact that the funding for holding the festival comes from donations given by every household and the banquets

Figure 5.2 The local temple is beautifully decorated during the *poi* festival

are held on the temple ground. A *poi chong* makes it an important occasion for joint participation by the various households in the village to effect repairs, cleaning and making the temple beautiful as well as preparing food for the parties.

During the past decade *poi chong* has become a traditional event that various villages arrange on a grand scale to which guests from outside the village are invited and has begun to assume the nature of competition between villages in the vicinity to see who can arrange a grander event. If Lak Chang happens in the previous year to have held a festival that was very grand and was the talk of people in the area, then next year nearby Fa Pho village would try to arrange a bigger and more colourful festival in order to surpass the other villages and make them lose face; so *poi* festivals have to be bigger and grander each successive year. The manner in which *poi* festivals are celebrated by the Tai has begun to change from being activities that stress competing for social prestige between different households in the same village, to becoming competitions for prestige and eminence between villages.

Death and Life-Cycle Rituals

The Tai Daikong give importance to changes according to life cycles by performing rituals and celebrating important occasions in a grand way for the three phases of life, namely: birth, marriage and death. We have already described rituals relating to birth and marriage in Chapter 3, so this part will highlight rituals that relate only to death and funeral preparations.

The thoughts and feelings of the Tai people regarding death have been influenced by Buddhism, particularly as regards reincarnation in various lives according to the laws of karma. Death in Tai cosmology is therefore something like an occasion for enhancing one's position or status in the pyramid of merit. The Tai firmly believe that if they accumulate merit by consistently fostering religion, observing the precepts and giving alms, they will definitely be born again in a status higher than their previous existence. For this reason, on approaching middle age, the Tai prefer to "prepare oneself" for death by regularly visiting temples to listen to sermons, observing the precepts, practising meditation, making merit and participating in religious rites. Tais in general look at death not as a fearsome occasion but merely as a passage to a state higher than the present one. To die peacefully at the appropriate age is therefore an ordinary happening, but death due to an epidemic or an illness lasting over a lengthy period are the doings of evil spirits.[16] Moreover, death due to brutal attacks, such as being stabbed to death or being murdered are the results of evil deeds accumulated from the previous life. The Tai believe that the soul of a woman who dies while in the state of pregnancy and during childbirth, will turn into an evil spirit, so rituals must be performed to prevent the evil spirit from coming back to haunt her husband and relatives by cutting open the abdomen and removing the dead child. The corpses of the child and the mother should be wrapped in mats and buried apart from each other so that the souls of the two persons shall not meet, and also to prevent this woman from having to encounter such bad luck again in her next life.

When someone dies in the village, his or her relatives will help to bathe the body meticulously clean, dress the corpse in the finest suit[17] and put a silver coin in the mouth as the fee for the boatman to send the soul of the deceased to a blissful place. The corpse is put into a coffin with the head turned towards the north; the body then lies in the house to allow relatives and neighbours to come by and pay final respects to the deceased, according to custom.

In customary practice, the Tai hold funeral rites for three days, and throughout these three days neighbours, relatives and friends will visit and offer condolences to the family of the host. Repasts are provided throughout these three days to entertain visitors who come to pay respects to the deceased. Visitors who join in the ceremony usually make token donations to defray expenses for the food. Some family relatives may bring articles of use—including money—and hand them over to the host family who will collect the money and various things for donation to the temple on behalf of the deceased after the burial ceremony. During all the three days' wake, the front of the house will be attended by young men beating long drums, gongs and firing off crackers at intervals to scare away demons that come to prey on the soul of the person who has just died, to entice or trick it into following the demons away to other places. Within the house, the host will set up tables of food to treat guests who come to pay respects to the deceased. Guests will take turns to express sorrow on his passing away and recall

---

16 Milne (1910:179).

17 In old times a corpse was dressed with the opening of the jacket to the back, instead of being fastened in front in the usual way. The reason for this custom was the belief that the spirit escaped from the back of the body.

his goodness and his benevolent character. Unlike funerals of the Thai people, no *chao chong* or priest is invited to say prayers at the ceremonies of the Tai.

On completion of three days, the host family will transport the deceased for burial at the village cemetery, an astrologer having been consulted in advance as to the auspicious hour for moving and burial. At the auspicious hour for moving the body, some five or six musicians striking drums and gongs and playing pipe instruments will lead the procession, followed by a group of male relatives acting as pall-bearers, the coffin having been placed on a wooden litter and covered with a funerary tower similar to funerals of the northern Thai people. Descendants and close relatives walk behind the coffin, followed by friends and neighbours proceeding in the direction of the cemetery. Tai villagers usually select a nearby hillside as the site for the village cemetery which has carved stones in the shape of a coffin and stone slabs engraved with names of the dead, similar to the "*huang sui*" or burial place of the Han Chinese.

If the deceased is a single woman who has not married, her relatives will take the coffin and tap it against trees during the procession to the cemetery[18] in the belief that in her next life she will not be so unfortunate as to die before having been married. Should the deceased be a person of affluence, the funeral tower and the procession will have exquisite and elaborate decorations; the spire of the tower will be adorned with metal fretwork sheets of beautiful patterns whilst the coffin will be covered with cloth embroidered with designs of dancing angels.

On arrival of the funeral procession at the cemetery, the monk who is already waiting at the grave will start the prayer rites for sending the soul of the dead person to the blissful world. Women generally do not climb up the hill to the cemetery but wait down below whilst the men carry the coffin up and lay it into the grave while the *chao chong* is praying. Normally the head of the dead will be turned towards the north, to help the spirit of the dead begin his journey to Mount Meru, the abode of God and great spirits. Inside the coffin, it is customary to place uncooked rice, tea and tobacco as rations for the deceased to carry on the way. After burial has been completed and a stone slab inscribed with the dead person's name has been erected, children or relatives of the deceased will set up a tray of food as propitiation and burn silver paper and gold paper to send

---

18 In traditional Tai cosmology, the tree was looked upon as an emblem of fertility, cf. Milne (1910:94).

to the soul of the deceased.[19] Thereafter, on completion of seven days after death, the family of the deceased will once again give a feast in the belief that on completion of seven days the spirit of the deceased will return to the house to say farewell for the last time. Descendants, relatives and close friends will gather at this ceremony to propitiate the spirit of the deceased. This propitiation marks the end of the funeral rites.

Life Crises Rituals

Calendrical rituals are arranged with feelings of piety. They are celebrations to commemorate important religious anniversaries, whilst cyclical rituals are those that have been arranged for a person or a community to adjust to the changing stations in life. Both calendrical rituals and cyclical rituals display the nature of expressive feelings shown collectively by a community or a large number of people, whilst crisis rituals are those with clearly instrumental aims or which must be for a certain purpose, such as to remedy a calamity, an adversity or for the purpose of escaping from a critical situation in life.

The causes and occasions of crisis may emanate from natural conditions, for instance, diseases of some type, accidents, drought or robbers plundering property. Such crises may be remedied by various methods, such as digging a canal to solve the problem of drought, posting guards to watch out for thieves, consulting a doctor to cure the malady, but certain crises cannot be corrected with reason or methods in the normal way, such as a prolonged illness that cannot be cured and persists in spite of hospital treatment. In such cases, explanations of life's crises may be somewhat different from the ordinary and normal reasons, such as this person may have been maliciously attacked (by spirits), or sometimes the explanation for the life crisis may derive from the influence of destiny and of the stars. For example: there was a man of middle age named Yee. This Lak Chang villager had to face drastic life crises in the interval of a few years; he fell ill many times and, after recovering from the latest bout, his young wife met an untimely death. Yee went to consult an astrologer in the village and got the explanation that the bad luck was because his house was not auspicious and was in conflict with his horoscope; he must move out to escape from the life crises.

---

19 Many elements of the Tai burial rite have been borrowed from the Han Chinese.

On such premises, some of life's crises such as chronic illnesses, natural calamities, accidents or bad luck of certain types cannot be remedied by normal means but must rely on supernatural measures of which there are at least four forms: astrology or predictions by horoscope; propitiating spirits to stop taunting and making mischief; the use of incantations, sorcery or employment of other propitious objects; and the performance of Buddhist religious rituals.

That the stars have influence over the lives of human beings is deeply rooted in the way of thinking and cosmology of the Tai people. Without access to the day, month, year of birth and actual moment of delivery used in determining his horoscope, a Tai barely has anything left to cope with his life, whether it concerns giving a name, choosing a life partner or even simple things, such as having a haircut or trimming nails. His life would be left only with confusion and complications because of inability to read his horoscope which is like a compass needle directing his life path. The Tai believe that the stars or the position of the various stars at the actual delivery time at birth and the movements of the stars at a later time have influence over the luck or misfortune that occur in the life of every human being. For this reason, various acts when done correctly according to auspicious hours will bear good results and conversely if performed at the wrong time or during an interval that is not propitious will have adverse results later on. Life is lived under auspicious and inauspicious planets and planetary constellations whose influence on human affairs is self-evident to all Tais.

Omens, like planetary constellations, may augur either good or bad consequences. Bad omens include a number of major types. Prominent among them is belief in the evil effect of a wild animal entering a place of human habitation, especially a house. Should one find a vulture or a crow perched on the house roof, it is an indication that its occupants may meet with bad luck. If reptiles crawl into the house, the Tai people believe that this is a bad omen signifying that the house-owner will lose property or may have bad luck in his trading. When Ai, an old woman in Lak Chang of some 70 years died, neighbours spread rumours that she had discovered a large beehive on a tree branch in front of the house and on the very same day a crow alighted on the house roof. Many neighbours warned her that this was a bad omen and urged her to go and consult an astrologer or to move out and sleep somewhere else temporarily, but she refused and therefore met the end of her life a couple of days later. Belief in things like horoscopes, the influence of the stars and luck make the Tai people often consult astrologers prior to engaging in any activities in order to check their horoscope and determine a propitious time, particularly for important acts in life, such as giving names, marriage, house-building and funerals.

When danger occurs in life, such as being knocked down by a car, being inflicted with a disease of unknown cause or which could not be cured, or encountering persistent bad luck time and again, then a Tai will choose to visit a medium for assistance in finding out the cause of the crisis that is afflicting his life, whether it was he himself or someone in the house who has done something that enraged an evil spirit. The medium will sit in meditation to discover the cause and to recommend remedial measures, such as recommending that the afflicted person erect a shrine with offerings to beg forgiveness from the spirit. Sometimes, the medium may suggest other techniques for fooling the spirit, such as changing one's name, moving away temporarily, feigning death and asking relatives to display a mock funeral. Such techniques are ruses to trick the demon into thinking that its victim is already dead and to eventually stop its taunts and attacks.

According to Tai beliefs, bad luck, illnesses and various crises emanate from karma that cannot be eliminated by propitiating spirits or by other methods or techniques but can be offset only by performing religious rituals and making merit and giving alms. In resolving life's problems, the Tai people turn to Buddhist rituals for protection against all other types of supernaturally caused dangers. For instance, to avert the dangers caused by planetary influence and terrestrial omens, the most effective defence is to build a *kongmu* or pagoda and to arrange for a *poi* festival to present Buddha statues and various articles to the temple. Other rituals performed in order to avert an impending calamity include the use of Buddhist sacra, spells and the practice of meditation, while others consist of the practice of alms such as redeeming the life of an animal that is going to be killed, making vows before a sacred Buddha image, saying prayers, observing the precepts and dedicating oneself to enter the priesthood if one escapes from the crisis or dangerous malady.

Furthermore, the Tai people also have various ways to cope with life's twists and turns and uncertainties by the use of necromancy, occultism and cabalistic inscriptions to achieve self-immunity, to obtain protection against snakes and for creating magnetic attraction and charisma, including the use of various charms and talismans as well as implanting rolled leaf amulets on the arms and legs.

For the Tai Daikong, occultism, propitiating spirits and the employment of sorcery or black magic in various forms are inseparable from Buddhist religious tenets.

The Tai believe that the incantations, occultism and the spirits are always subjected to the laws of karma according to the Buddhist faith. Buddhism, spiritualism and occultism are tangibly present in the roles of the *chao chong* who officiates in Buddhist rites and frequently acts as astrologer and inscribes magical tattoos as well. For this reason, belief in spirits, Buddhism and occultism are intermingled as one and inseparable in the viewpoints, beliefs and rituals of the Tai Daikong.

Beliefs, Rituals and Social Change

During the past few decades, although Buddhism has still played an important role in the life and culture of the Tai village society, changes in the economy and social pattern in several aspects, especially the expansion of the market economy and the rapid increase in demand for agricultural products, have resulted in inevitable variation in the beliefs and rituals of the Tai Daikong, whether they are changes in the roles of the temples and monks, merit-making or performances of rituals in the social life of the Tai.

In former days, a Tai would treat a monk or *chao chong* with reverence. A monk is ranked as a "noble", not as an ordinary man, but as a special person who has an important role in performing religious rituals, a teacher of books, an adviser of the community on various matters and the pivot of merit-making and alms-giving of all types. In a society where right living according to the Buddhist teaching is of extreme importance, the way of life of the monk is the ideal in the scale of values of the Tai. Thus the monk is revered in the capacity of one who fosters the Buddhist religion, an ideal model of moral standard and life conduct; the *chao chong* is the children's mentor, counsellor of the village head, a spiritual guide for the elderly and also a mediator in disputes and discord within the

Figure 5.3 A Buddhist monk in Na Muu village, Muang Khon

community.[20] Villagers should show respect to the *chao chong* by kneeling or squatting on the floor in polite attitude when facing him, and provide support in matters of food and other necessities for maintaining the monkhood.

During the past few decades, the role of the *chao chong* clearly began to decline. Schools began to replace the temples and the *chao chong's* duties as a teacher decreased. During the period of the Cultural Revolution, many temples in Daikong were destroyed and the *chao chong* were apprehended and disrobed. Although during the past ten years or so, continuous renovations, repairs and rebuilding of temples have been done to replace the old ones, the values of being ordained as a monk began to decline from the viewpoint of the Tai. Strenuous agricultural production resulting from a constant attempt to keep pace with growing market demands, as well as the strict birth-control policy have caused the demand for labour in the agricultural sector to multiply. The importance of

20 Pattaya (1959:284–287).

encouraging sons to devote themselves to studies and to the preparation for ordination has quickly declined. Many temples, including the Lak Chang village temple, remain without a resident *chao chong*. The absence of *chao chong* inadvertently began to put an end to the required officiating role of the *chao chong* at religious rituals.

Furthermore, merit-making of the Tai people began to show a downward trend. In former days, occasions for merit-making and alms-giving were the main incentives for the Tai people to save up money to accumulate merits and virtue for the next world.[21] In times past, the Tai people considered that a person who did a lot of merit-making was a good person, honourable and highly regarded socially. However, at the present time, the values of the Tai regarding merit-making have begun to change. *Poi* festivals have now become activities which the whole village joins in arranging, in order to compete with other villages. Within the village itself, the Tai now lay stress on worldly matters, such as marriage and funeral ceremonies by spending lavishly and incurring huge expenses for arranging such events. Although Buddhist beliefs and rituals still prevail as important influences in the way of thinking, the traditional customs and daily life of the Tai, economic and trading activities have gradually become more and more important in the lifestyle and culture of the Tai Daikong.

---

21 Tien (1986:74–96).

Chapter Six

GENDER ROLES AND GENDER RELATIONS

The gender roles and gender relations in Tai village society have been dominated by norms and values as well as religious beliefs and an ideology of power that clearly define the status and duties of a man and a woman in the capacity of a child, husband and wife. Social norms reflect ideals or expectations, but in real life the relationship between man and woman, husband and wife, may be more complicated than idealistic models, as there can be haggles and conflicts, and they may change according to economic turns, cultural adaptation and individual adjustment. In this chapter, we will examine the gender roles and gender relations in Tai village society and special emphasis will be placed on the contrast between the ideals and the changes taking place in the daily life of a Tai farming community.

Gender Roles in Tai Culture

In the Tai cosmology, a man stands on a higher stage of existence than a woman.[1] Being nearer to perfection, he enjoys a higher status of merit than a woman or, to put it plainly, the Tai believe that a man is more blessed than a woman. This notion is influenced by Buddhist religious teachings which allows only men the right to be ordained a monk, together with the viewpoint that a man is more gifted, both physically and spiritually, than a woman. Only men can reach

---

1 Milne (1910:31).

Nirvarna or become a Buddha.[2] Nevertheless, a woman's role within the family and community is accepted to be no less important than that of a man. A daughter is cherished and regarded as a source of delight and happiness to her parents no less than a son. The social roles of women have been prescribed by tradition to shoulder the responsibilities of cooking food and child-rearing. Consequently, a woman's duties are heavier than those of a man, since she works in the field as much as a man and still has to perform household chores, look after the children and also take care of the trading side. So a woman is busy with work for almost the entire day. The pictures of a woman toiling on the farm land, carrying vegetables home to boil pig-feed, loading farm produce on the farm utility van to sell at Muang Khon market, spoon-feeding her children or busy doing kitchen work are sights that one will come upon any day on walking through a Tai village. It is rarely that we see a group of women sitting around or spending leisure time chatting in convivial groups like their male counterparts. Even at functions arranged for marriages, funerals or *poi* festivals which should be a time to relax, women are still the ones to do the heavy work of cooking food and preparing for the social gatherings.

Figure 6.1 Tai women at the open market in Muang Khon

---

[2] Brant (1956:650), quoted in Pattaya (1959:193).

Even though a woman works more heavily than a man, and has to bear greater responsibilities than a man, Tai social values dictate that it is the man who is head of a household and enjoys a higher social status. A Tai woman will be taught and trained from childhood to be respectful and obedient to her father and, after leaving the household following marriage, to also be respectful and obedient to her husband. Tradition requires that a woman displays respectful manners towards a man.[3] A daughter or wife may not eat before the father; normally, household members, both male and female, will eat together but on occasions where guests are present, the women—especially the daughters—have to be in attendance and prepare the food trays for the father and guests and thereafter to withdraw and eat separately.[4] A woman should not interrupt men in a conversation circle since it is considered bad manners.

Established norms requiring that a woman should be responsible for housework, rearing children and also the main labour in the ricefields, may have evolved from ancient traditions that a boy needed to spend the greater part of his time studying in temples whilst a girl did not have much opportunity for book learning but had instead to stay at home and help her mother do the housework. Thus the Tai male received better education, and was able to read and write whilst a woman did not have the same opportunity for studies and education. For this reason, the Tai in olden days held the view that women were less knowledgeable and should be the ones that had to listen to men, since men had studied the scriptures and were therefore more intelligent.

As a Tai male had to spend a great proportion of time studying for ordination, in travelling to different places for trading, being conscripted by the *chaopha* for warfare or for labour, the Tai male had rather less time to stay at home than the womenfolk. Thus a woman was the main source of labour for the household as well as for production on the farms, in stock raising and looking after domestic affairs. Being the main labour force has given women considerable bargaining power in the family as can be seen from the Tai woman's freedom in choosing a life partner. A Tai woman is able to save and accumulate money that she has earned by her own efforts, such as weaving and basket work.[5]

---

3 Tien (1986:55).
4 Milne (1910:117).
5 cf. Pattaya (1959:195–196).

Nowadays, as schools have replaced the temples in terms of providing education, boys and girls have to learn on rather the same footing, so there is now no disparity between young Tai men and women in their ability to read and write. This is despite the fact that women still shoulder heavy work as before by having to accept the responsibilities of house-keeping, raising children, farm work, not to mention running the business side and controlling home expenses as well. The role that women perform in trading the family products in the Muang Khon market has rewarded them with a higher social standing. Experience gained as vendors in the market has turned Tai housewives into experts in bargaining prices with merchants, so they are usually assigned the task of negotiating prices of products with the Han traders who come to buy wheat, melons and other agricultural products in the village. After negotiations on prices between the merchant and the housewife are concluded, she will tell the buyer to formally settle the deal once again with her husband.[6] The present-day Tai woman's important roles in production, control, marketing and managing the household economy have resulted in raising her social standing to a higher level than before. The women of Lak Chang now unequivocally agree that men and women stand more and more on equal terms. Tai women enjoy a higher standing compared to their Han sisters who, on marriage, also take up their husbands' family name, but their roles in production and their bargaining power on the social scale are less than those of Tai women. Furthermore, the endogamous marriage rule which encourages marriages between young people in the same village has enabled the woman to continue holding on to social ties with her family of orientation. A woman is not abandoned to fare for herself, but she has allies and a family group always ready to offer her continuous assistance, the more so when she leaves the family to live independently with her husband and children, when the influence of her mother-in-law begins to decline. In such circumstances, a woman who is a wife is able to expand her role in matters of production, trading and supervision over the family's economic affairs with greater convenience.

The significance of endogamous marriage, the blessing and approval of the village elders which are required if the couple demand the right to a share of farmland later on, as well as the benefits of holding marriage ceremonies and having grand parties—all these factors have helped to enhance the role and standing of women.

---

6 A number of husbands interviewed agreed that their wives are shrewd businesswomen, highly skilled in bargaining for a better price for farm produce.

In a marriage, the groom has to pay bridewealth to the woman's family, must be responsible for expenses in arranging a party, has to be the side that goes to beg the woman to marry him. The bride's family is also in a position to demand a higher bridewealth for their daughter. The parents of the woman usually hold back a portion of the bridewealth for their daughter, to be presented at the ceremony of giving a name to the first grandchild.

The Tai village society has no tradition of discrimination against women, such as the old Chinese custom of binding the feet of young girls, of covering the face or other prohibitions that restrict the freedom or hinder women from seeking success in life. At present a Tai woman is likely to have an equal opportunity to any man if she wants to continue her education in high school or institutes of higher learning in Muang Khon or Kunming. A sizeable number of Tai women are now beginning to enter new professions, as teachers, nurses, doctors or government officials. Freedom in choosing careers is much greater than in the past.

However, the concept, with its roots embedded in religious beliefs, that man is the master, has not entirely disappeared but still exercises its influence on the way of thinking of both men and women and still plays an important part in determining the gender roles and gender relationships in the Tai village community.

The Concept of Male Supremacy

Although Tai women presently have a more complicated role and higher social standing than before and despite the remarkable extent of sexual equality in Tai society—remarkable not only by contrast with the status of women in Asia, but also with significant segments of the contemporary West—it is nevertheless a basic premise of Tai culture that men are naturally and inherently superior to women. Even though the concept of male supremacy is present in various cultures throughout the world, such as in China,[7] India,[8] Middle East[9] or Thai[10] cultures and cannot be considered as a new phenomenon in any way, the reasons given to explain male supremacy still vary from culture to culture.

---

7 Hsu (1963).
8 Kapadia (1966).
9 Patai (1971).
10 Yos (1992).

In Daikong, the primary reason offered to explain male supremacy concerns merit and the law of karma. The Tai believe that men possess a certain innate essence which invests its possesser with superior moral, intellectual and spiritual qualities to women. The Tai cite the superiority of the male, not for reasons of bodily strength or physical stamina or ability in doing work, but for superiority of intellect and of the spirit.

Hence, however proficient a female may be in matters of production, trading, profit-sharing, education or management of a household economy, she will always have a lower potential than a male on the spiritual side. She is more distant from heaven or Nirvana than the male.

The belief in male spiritual supremacy is not confined only to men. On the contrary, this belief and way of thinking is held strongly by women as well. Sharing the belief in male spiritual supremacy, women recite the following conventional prayer:

> Before attaining Nirvana, I pray that I may be reborn as a male in the future existence. And I wish to be freed from this state of a woman, and when in future existences I pass through abodes of men and spirits, I wish to be born a man endowed with virtue, understanding and faith.[11]

When one is in the company of a female group in Lak Chang and asks the housewives and maidens what they would like to become in the next life, almost every one, particularly those who are already married, gives the same answer that they want to be born as a man and, if possible, as a man of affluence. The women of Lak Chang not only desire to be born as a man because of spiritual superiority, but because they see that a male enjoys a happier life than a female, shoulders less of a work burden than a female and has more time to himself in seeking personal enjoyment. On the other hand, the life of a female has to meet greater hardship and heavier responsibilities, has to face worrisome physical problems from monthly periods, pregnancy, the throes of childbirth, has to be a slave of her children and husband until old age. A woman's life has only suffering that comes from her physical nature added with work duties that are heavier than those of a man; so to be born a female is not so delightful and, if one could choose, Tai women would speak unanimously that they would prefer to be born a man.

---

11 Pe Maung Tin (1961:418), quoted in Spiro (1977:260).

The belief in male supremacy is also apparent in the shape of various symbols in Tai culture, such as the peacock which has beautiful feathers and the long drum which men beat at various traditional events. The male sex symbols have been used as ethnic symbols. Male superiority is also shown in other tangible forms, for instance the seating of a male or the father at a dinner table; the father's chair will be towards the north, which is the direction pointing towards Mount Meru which is auspicious. The belief in the spiritual superiority of men is symbolically projected onto inanimate objects. Thus, the northern side of the house is the noble side, and it is the side on which the men sit. The southern side is the ignoble side, it is the side on which the women sit.

Even though male superiority is presented as being derived from the real inner force that is greater than that of the female, the nucleus of the superior male human being has been fostered and developed to higher potential by completion of studies for ordination into priesthood, which only males are allowed. The male's innate superiority enables him to become a monk, which in turn increases his already pronounced superiority over the female. In Tai religious rituals, elders and male groups will sit near the monks and Buddhist statues in the temple whilst females are seated hindmost. After the feast of the monks has ended, males will then eat first while females will eat afterwards.

Male superiority is also manifest in other social activities, for instance in marriages. In former days a man might have several wives, or should the wife pass away and the husband want to marry again, he was free to arrange marriage ceremonies and parties every time he desired; but a widow who wished to marry again was not entitled to demand any bridewealth or to arrange any marriage ceremony.

A female enjoys a lower social status than a male and in actual fact a female on her own has no status in society. She enjoys social status only by being a daughter or wife of a man. Hence a female's social status is near that of a child; in other words, no status, no prestige, no social recognition.

Male chauvinism reflects the roots of basic ways of thinking from ancient times which sees the male as having greater sanctity than the female. Consequently a wife must look up to and respect her husband next to other sacred entities such as the Lord Buddha, the holy precepts, monks, elders and parents. Sanctity unites the male with the Buddhist religion and priests whilst the female is the surrogate at medium sessions or spirit propitiating rites, and this is one of the other important reasons that the Tai male uses to explain why virtually all the mediums in practically every Tai farm village are females.

Females are also looked upon as the unclean sex and the source of ecological disasters. Menstruation of the female is an unclean thing and may cause cabalistic inscriptions, various enchanted articles or auspicious states of things to lose their original powers. For this reason, the Tai have a taboo against a man touching a woman during her menstrual period or having sex with a woman undergoing medical treatment or arranging *poi* festivals at that time in the belief that it will cause ecological problems and will not be auspicious.

Nowadays such taboos are beginning to be discarded and the concept of male supremacy is being undermined by women's increasing roles and bargaining powers including changes in various aspects of cultural tradition. Yet the beliefs and many taboos concerning sexual contacts and pollution of the female body still remain and may be proof of the existence of a certain uneasiness as well as perturbations that males entertain against females—the fear of being overwhelmed by the wife.

In real life, the Tai male takes it most seriously if teased by friends that he is afraid of his wife or is a henpecked husband. Every Tai man believes that the woman who is his wife will try by every and all means to have power over him and will try to control his life. Women control men by the use of endearments, seductions and sex including the use of love potions and magical incantations. The fear of coming under the control of women has made almost every Tai man have uneasy and contradictory feelings about women. Tai men view women as the gender that attracts, arouses emotions and feelings or, in plain words, they see women as a sex object that they should seek and keep. Conversely Tai men are afraid of women, afraid of being dominated and subjugated. Paradoxically, men see themselves by nature as superior to women, but they open the way for women to share equally or to even have greater roles than men as regards production and trading. Men have to depend upon their wives for cooking food, looking after the house and raising children, and women are the ones that have real power in the family.

Viewed this way, the concept of male superiority may be a self-preservation mechanism created to protect the male from fear of the female, from fear of being suppressed and fear of challenges from the female. The concept of male superiority has helped the male to be dependent on the female although in actuality it is the female that has power to make decisions and who controls the male.

Gender Roles and Social Expectations

Male supremacy in the religious sphere seems to reflect the belief that the male is a sacred being relative to the female. And since men are superior to women, it is therefore proper, according to Tai cultural norms, that the husband should have greater power than the wife. Traditional cultural norms demand that the husband should be older than the wife for the simple reason that, according to Tai custom, a person who is younger must show respect to an older person. Husbands, therefore, should be of greater age because it is to the husband that the wife must show respect in his capacity as the wife's provider and protector. Similarly, the wife must honour and obey the husband, administer to his comforts and strictly obey the husband's orders, to be faithful to the husband and ensure that he is "living well".

In Tai marriage ceremonies, when the groom goes to receive the bride back home and pay respects to the village elder, the latter will give a lesson on "the duties" and responsibilities of husband and wife towards each other as follows: The duties of the man or husband are (1) to be the provider of the family, (2) to be diligent, to have endurance, to be willing to face hard work, (3) to conduct life smoothly, not to become addicted to excessive drinking and gambling habits, and (4) to treat his wife with love and compassion, refrain from beatings or the use of force or threats. On the other hand the duties of a good woman or wife are: (1) to be a good housewife, look after the home, cook food, look after the children, care for the comforts of her husband, (2) to be diligent in work, not be lazy, to stay at home and not roam about the village unnecessarily, (3) to take wise care of the family money and be frugal, and (4) to be faithful to her husband, not be arrogant or show interest in other men but only in her husband.

The social expectations regarding the ideal roles of husband and wife are values which the majority of villagers, particularly those already married with a family, agree to be suitable.[12] Should one examine these social expectations, it would be obvious that most of the attributes of the ideal wife reflect the ideology of male supremacy. It should be noticed that the issue of fidelity of the married couple

---

12 Data on gender roles and social expectations are derived from interviews with 24 married villagers. Twelve men and twelve women were asked to describe the qualities which constitute a good husband and a good wife and to specify their duties to each other. Most men and women gave almost identical responses to these questions.

touches upon the role of the wife only whilst, for the husband, social expectations do not stress fidelity to the wife at all. The reason for this disparity may be because the Tai believe that men by nature do not know how to master their feelings in sexual matters. Interest in women is part of a male's inborn trait; deviations, extra conjugal pursuits whenever the opportunity offers are part of manliness and normal things. Infidelity of a husband outside the village is neither unexpected nor threatening to the wife, whereas any sexual misconduct on the wife's part is not only a serious moral breach, but is highly threatening to her husband. Therefore a good wife should not roam about the village unnecessarily, particularly at night time because, in so doing, she would be the target of malicious gossip, leading to quarrels with her husband because the wife did not make use of her time in looking after the house, in cooking and taking full care of her husband's comforts.

Aside from the issue of fidelity, the other good qualities of the husband and wife are of similar attributes, whether they refer to diligence or enduring hard work. Both husband and wife are expected to be diligent in earning a living, know how to save money and not be extravagant in spending. The wife especially is expected to manage the family income and expenditure competently.

According to social expectation, the husband is the family breadwinner whilst the wife is the good housewife. Food is an important symbol of Tai society that binds the husband, wife and family members together. Food and feasts are important components of *poi* festivals, marriage ceremonies, funerals and ceremonies of almost all kinds in Tai society. In married life, the husband is the one who "obtains food" for the family while the wife is the one who "prepares" the food. A good husband has to find food to feed the family and a good wife has to prepare food for her husband to have a full stomach at every meal. Food is the symbol of exchange of benefits and mutual amelioration. Therefore, in the event of a heated and vehement quarrel, the wife may stop cooking food for her husband or refuse to eat together with her husband as a protest or to express dissatisfaction, which is the only form of protest that the wife is able to make to the husband.

A model wife must not only cook and see to the comforts of her husband but must also honour and display respectful obedience to her husband. When in the midst of friends, relatives or strangers, the wife has to especially be in attendance and at the service of her husband, but not join in the conversation if not invited and she should not express opinions on any subject unless the husband first asks her to do so. That a child shows respect to an elder and the wife shows respect to her husband are considered as norms of social order in Tai society.

Even though, in the formal setting, the wife is the one that honours the husband, most Tai women are well aware of their powers and influence within the households. A Tai female, according to the view of one elder in Lak Chang, "puts her words and decisions in the mouth of the husband, lets him be the one that declares her decisions".

For this reason, we have to differentiate clearly between formal dominance and actual dominance in the husband and wife relationship. In Tai village society, the formal relationship between husband and wife exhibits all the patterns of deference and respect required by the cultural norms of male supremacy. The male may receive the place of honour as the head of the family—the formal decision-maker on family matters—but more often than not we find that the real power and leadership are in the hands of the wife. From studies of husband and wife relationships in Lak Chang, we discover rather clearly that the wife has a higher role and influence than the husband in nearly every household. It is the woman who is the real leader of the family. On asking for the opinion of some 20 couples as to who is the real leader of the household, every couple unanimously agreed that the husband is the family leader. But on questioning *other* households as to who they think is the family head, the answers we received from over 80 per cent of couples turned out to be that the wife was the real family leader. It can be seen that when we asked the husband and wife to consider their status role in their household, the husband and wife answered the question based on cultural norms and social expectations—saying that the husband is the household leader—but when we asked other families to consider the role and standing, the opinion we received reflects the true social relationship. On top of that, when we asked the opinion of some four or five elders in Lak Chang during a conversation at a *poi* festival, the elders gave a jocular reply that the majority of Tai males, including the elders of Lak Chang, are all under the supervision and care of their wives.

Dominance between husband and wife in a household is an ambiguity, easily leading to misunderstanding. We tend to use the word dominance in the sense of control or one party having to accept the authority of the other party. However, the state of leading or having power in a household can mean the ability to steer the mind, influencing or coaxing the other party by various means into accepting one's ideas. In the family context, dominance by the husband or the wife usually means the ability to control, persuade or coax the other party into complying with his or her wishes.

In real life, the power of the wife may not be formally evident since the husband receives the honour and respect in the presence of friends or guests. The male has his own seat and is the one to dine before his wife, is seated near the monk in the temple, for instance, but the power of the wife is clearly evident in the choice of crops to be planted in the following year, in fixing and bargaining the price of produce, in managing the income and expenditure of the household, which are of greater importance than official leadership status. Moreover, the area that shows clearly and tangibly the power of the wife in the household is her role as manager of the household economy. Household expenses are under the control of the wife and even the head of the family must ask for money from his wife to spend on personal business.

For these reasons, we can say that the issue of dominance in the husband and wife relationship is rather ambiguous. In terms of cultural norms, the Tai male holds a higher position than his wife: he is the household chief, receives honour and respectful obedience from his wife; the husband walks in front whilst the wife follows; the wife is the first to rise and the last to sleep; the male speaks at village meetings whilst the wife may sit quietly listening or stay at home and not join the meeting. At the same time, if we were to look at performances within the family context, we would instead find that the wife takes the leading role in agricultural production and management of the household. The Tai people accept that the female has greater responsibility and authority in making decisions regarding household affairs than the male and, normally, household affairs also include production management, trading and control over the entire income and expenditure of the household. To that extent, the wife is dominant in the family.

For the Tai male of Lak Chang, power and dominance within the household are of little significance because they pertain to worldly matters only, while in the things that really count—that is, in spiritual matters—it is the husband who is dominant. The Tai female also agrees that her authority in the household and in managing production just "add responsibilities" and put a burden on her shoulders. Even though wives have higher roles and bargaining powers as well as social standing than before, the women view their extra responsibilities as extra drudgery and sufferings. For these reasons, a Tai female would still like to be born again as a man because she sees that a male does not have to shoulder such great responsibilities.

Anyhow, even though the Tai, both male and female alike, look at the authority of the female as being unimportant, the female as controller of the money purse is the deciding factor in having control over the husband and his dependence on her. In accepting the duties of supervising the household money, the wife is able to have control over the husband within her household.

Within the family, the wife controls her husband. Outside the family, in the domain of symbolic power such as religious affairs and local politics, the husband controls his wife. The husband is the one who manipulates the religious symbols, supervises merit-making rituals and controls the tokens of power. However, within the perimeter of household and economic activities, the male is the one who is managed and controlled by the female from the day he is born to the day he dies. From infancy to youth, the Tai male is under his mother's control and when he marries and has a family of his own, he is under his wife's control.

The obverse of the wife's control of the husband is the husband's dependence on the wife. Of the villagers of Lak Chang whom we interviewed, almost all of them explained that the wife is the one who controls the household's finance because *the husband wants her to perform this duty*. The male wants to have a wife who is able to supervise and take responsibility for the household's finances capably. In taking over these tasks, the wife is well aware of her authority within the household and the dependence of the husband on her. Some Tai women denied that taking over the supervision and management of the family purse was the decisive factor for control of the husband but explained that they found it necessary to look after the household's finance because *the male is irresponsible* and if the husband was allowed to manage, he might squander all the household's money on gambling, loafing and various frivolities. For these reasons, it was necessary for the female to take charge of the household's finance. Some Tai women explained the reason for them accepting responsibility for the household's money from a different angle. They explained that they accepted responsibility for taking care of the household's finance because of *the love they have for their husband.* "If we allow our husband to spend money freely and extravagantly, he would have to work too hard." These are the two types of explanations that we heard most often when we questioned Tai housewives on the reason why women take over control of household finances.

The contradictions and inconsistencies between the cultural and structural dimension of the relationship between the sexes in Daikong are not uncommon when compared with a great number of peasant societies. Spiro[13] describes the wife's role in Burmese peasant society as the one that controls and makes decisions regarding almost all economic activities of the household whilst the man has formal authority outside the household boundary. In the same way, Hildred Geertz[14] has noted the gender roles of the Javanese peasant society thus:

> The wife makes most of the decisions; she controls all the family finances, and although she gives her husband formal deference and consults with him on major matters, it is usually she who is dominant. Strong-willed men may have a relationship of equal partnership with their wives, but families actually dominated by the man are exceedingly rare.

Similar forms of gender relationship are also reported in research on family life of Northern Thai peasants by Sulamith Potter.[15]

In Tai peasant society, the contrast between social ideals and reality regarding male and female roles is absorbed in the love and intimate ties that the husband and wife share between one another. Marriage built on love, mutual attraction and free will, as well as the fact that husband and wife work together in almost every aspect, has made the couple quite close to each other with occasions to chat and consult one another tending to create lasting mutual understanding.

Married life in Tai peasant society is usually peaceful. Divorces appear to be few and far between. In Lak Chang village, there has not been a divorce for over 20 years which, however, does not mean that there are no quarrels between husbands and wives. Quarrels and arguments between married couples occasionally occur in Tai peasant society as elsewhere. Arguments may sometimes

13 Spiro (1977:280–285).
14 Geertz (1961:46).
15 Potter (1976).

reach vehement stages so that a couple will refuse to speak to each other for days, or stop eating together, or the wife may cease preparing dishes for her husband as a sign of protest. Anyhow, quarrels between married couples seldom appear to become so violent as to resort to attacking one another. Tai villagers consider wife-beating as the way of vile people, despicable behaviour that is strongly condemned by the community.

Squabbles between husband and wife therefore are usually of a temporary nature and invariably end in reconciliation. The reasons for the rarity of divorces in the village can be attributed to several factors. The first one is that marriages between husband and wife arise from love; the young people choose their own life partners, so the union is based on love and mutual understanding from the start. Secondly, violent quarrels are not tolerated by the Tai community. When conflicts arise between individuals or groups, whether these are disagreements between husband and wife, between relatives or friends or between neighbours, the elders of the kin group act as mediators to quell the dispute before hostilities grow out of proportion and become irreparable. Thirdly, Tai people place special significance on image and prestige. Divorce brings shame and dishonour to the family name, so it is a thing to be avoided at all cost. Tai society does not accept a person that has divorced his or her spouse. Some elders say that both the men and women who have divorced usually have to live alone for the rest of their lives because nobody would want to marry such a person. Lastly, it is the family, not the individual, that is the unit of land holding. A divorce results in the family's extinction, creating a problem in the structure of land distribution followed by many other problematic situations. For the various reasons stated above, marriages and conjugal relationships between men and women in Tai peasant community tend to be of a lasting nature or, at least, there does not exist a case of divorce in Lak Chang for us to discern the reasons or to conclude otherwise.

Gender Roles in Changing Times

During the past four decades, Tai village society in Daikong has undergone changes in many aspects. The increase in the number of households has resulted in the land holding of each family decreasing in size. Population and birth control policies which have been strictly enforced have caused the family labour force to shrink whilst the demand for agricultural production has steadily increased, forcing the Tai peasants to work more heavily throughout the year to enable production to keep pace with market demand and to obtain cash income to meet rising costs of consumption of goods from outside. After four centuries of Chinese domination, the Tai people have come to accept many cultural characteristics of the Han as their own. Presently, the Tai favour building houses out of brick with tile roofing similar to the Chinese architecture. Tai males have begun to dress in the popular style of the Chinese, use clan names in the Chinese way and eat meals with chopsticks as the Chinese do.

Nowadays women play greater roles in production and trade, resulting in their enjoyment of higher standing and bargaining power in village society. Changes in women's roles have also caused gender relations in Tai society to follow suit. Tai females have begun to exercise the pivotal role in the family and the stabilising force of the community.

Anyone who has travelled to Muang Khon or other towns in Daikong may have noticed that it is difficult to tell the difference between present-day Tai villages and other Chinese villages in Yunnan province. Tai houses show almost no dissimilarity in appearance to houses of the Chinese. The body build, facial features and attire of the Tai are almost indistinguishable from the common Chinese. The outstanding feature or characteristic of the Tai at the present time is the dress of the Tai women. From childhood to youth, the style of dressing of the Tai maiden would not evidently be different from that of the Chinese. Teenage Tai girls favour T-shirts, jeans and high heels in the Chinese fashion. However, after marriage and having a home, every young Tai female turns to wearing black skirts, open front blouses, hair knotted in a bun with a bright coloured turban as the symbol of a married woman. Up to this day, Tai women still preserve this traditional style of dress which firmly distinguishes the Tai ethnic identity.

Tai women also play an important role in the preservation of Tai cultural identity. Strong and lasting ties between mother and daughter have enabled the mother to instil the sense of identity and motherhood into the daughter who has become the representative of the mother; the daughter becomes the mother's successor—the daughter is socialised to accept responsibilities for the back-breaking chores of the agricultural economy, child-rearing and household supervision. The reproduction of mothering in Tai society has become a unifying force that provides continuity and stability to the family and the community. Tai women continue to play a leading role in terms of production and reproduction of the sense of ethnic identity, which is the subject that will be described in detail in the next chapter.

Chapter Seven

CONTINUITY AND RECONSTRUCTION OF TAI ETHNIC IDENTITY

In the book *Islands of History*, Marshal Sahlins asserted that "culture is precisely the organization of the current situation in the terms of a past".[1] In other words, the past is always practised in the present, not because the past imposes itself, but because subjects in the present fashion the past in the practice of their social identity. Thus the organisation of the current situation in the terms of a past can only take place in the present. The past that affects the present and the future is a past constructed in the present. The imposition of a model of the past on the present occurs as a wilful act in socialisation and in nation-building, and in both cases the relation between the constitution of identity and the identification of the past is strongly systemic.[2]

The construction and reconstruction of identity is a complex temporal interaction of multiple practices of identification internal and external to a population. The making of history is thus an important part of the constitutive process of identity formation. "A society is what it remembers, we are what we remember..."[3] History is just as much a social construct as ethnic or group

1 Sahlins (1985:155).
2 Friedman (1994:141).
3 Wendt (1987:79).

identity. The attribution of meaning and production of identity models are motivated practices. History and identity should therefore be understood in terms of the way in which they are constructed and reconstructed.

During the past two decades, the construction and reconstruction of identity on the basis of "nation-state" have reached a critical stage in many countries. Old imagined communities based on citizenship of nation-states have begun to decline rapidly in importance under pressure from globalisation storms. New forms of imagined community based on primordial loyalties, ethnicity, local community, language and other culturally concrete forms have begun to play increasingly important roles.

On the disastrous collapse of the Soviet Empire, Soviet citizenship rapidly lost its meaning. The once mighty and fearsome empire disintegrated and faded away in the wake of rapid increase of ethnic-based movements for political and economic autonomy. Several ethnic groups, such as the Lithuanians and the Kazakstans, tried to break free from Russia. The process of fragmentation of the traditional political community has taken the form of ethnic movements toward local autonomy and community self-control. Each group united itself based on ethnic identity to struggle for the freedom to manage their own lives. What Clifford Geertz[4] depicted some years ago as the "integrative revolution" in reference to the so-called modernisation process in the new post-colonial states of the Third World might just as well be depicted today as the "disintegrative revolution" in reference to the system as a whole especially since the 1990s.[5]

The re-emergence and intensification of ethnic conflicts in various parts of the world such as the Basques and the Catalans in Spain, the Irish and Scots in the United Kingdom; the emergence of groups known as the Fourth World, such as Indians of North America, the Hawaiians in the United States, the Kastom movement of the Melanesians or of the Karens, Lawa and Tai in Burma; these ethnic conflicts are clear evidence of the process of fragmentation which has taken the form of ethnic movements for cultural autonomy. New imagined communities are being constructed on the bases of primordial loyalties, languages and ethnic identities. A kind of membership known as citizenship in territorially defined and state-governed societies or nation-states is being replaced by an identity based on other culturally concrete forms.

---

4 Geertz (1973).
5 Friedman (1994:86).

In cases where the population or "citizenship" in question is only weakly integrated into a larger political unit or a nation-state, an ethnic movement may simply imply political and economic autonomy in a situation where the ethnic group still manages to retain its own cultural and ethnic identity. This applies to groups such as the Tai and Kachin of Burma[6] and the Kurds in Iran.[7] In such movements, these groups may have been able to maintain their traditional niches in large political systems dating back to early colonial periods. These groups may have been able to maintain their distinct cultural heritage which is set apart from the rest of the nation-state's majority community. Consequently the struggle for self-determination and independence does not stress new ethnic identity and local culture since these groups already have their own cultural and historical continuity.

But in the cases of ethnic groups that have been assimilated and absorbed to some degree and have become a part of the nation-state, the ethnic identity which was based on the use of the same language, nationality, religion or certain cultural symbols would have greatest importance in creating a culturally distinct community when they break away or try to break away from the former nation-state. Creation of a new imagined community therefore involves the creation of a new self-identity based on a culture and/or an ethnic group quite separate from the former nation-state.

In the case of the Tai in Daikong, throughout the past several centuries, the local culture and identity have been very much taken for granted simply because there was no historical discontinuity between the present and the cultural past. However, after the Communist revolution in 1949, the abolition of the *chaopha* and the changes that took place in Daikong during the Cultural Revolution moved the Tai to alienate themselves from the larger political community. More than two decades of direct Chinese rule after the Cultural Revolution resulted in a crisis of identity, the re-emergence and intensification of sub-national ethnic conflicts and a search for meaning and cultural roots.

Ever since the early 1980s, after the political upheaval in China began to subside to a somewhat orderly condition, a search for cultural roots and a reconstruction of the Tai ethnic identity began to emerge in Daikong. The economic and

---

6 Leach (1954).
7 Friedman (1994:87).

political crises which the Tai people had to endure from the 1950s onwards made it necessary for them to have a new self-definition and new meaning to fit the real experiences facing them. Naturally, the process of self-definition of the Tai did not take place in a vacuum but sprang up in a world whose self-definition has already been predetermined at a certain level. For this reason, the reconstruction of ethnic identity was a process of separating ethnic boundaries and selecting certain past experiences and incidents to be rewritten so that they represent "life experiences" which connect the past with the present and the future. The self-definition process therefore means rewriting the "real history" of the group or a new historical chapter. History making is one form of the self-definition process as long as such history making links or reflects involvement between incidents alleged to have happened in the past with present living conditions. History making in the self-defining process therefore means the creation of a set of incidents that has meaning to people of the present generation.

During the past decade, the reconstruction of the Tai ethnic identity has become a matter of conscious choice. The Tai select their own histories which are significant events for them now, isolated from the mass of events that they have actually encountered. The Tai have been trying to reconstruct and reinterpret their own history by means of writing folklore and Tai chronicles, such as *The Tai Yai Chronicles* [8] and *Muang Tai Chronicles,* [9] which are interpretations of Tai chronicles from the original text of *Chaophya Dharmatay.* In these writings, including interpretations of other folklore of the Tai Daikong, the Tai people are telling themselves and other people that more than a thousand years ago there was an independent and self-governing Tai state that expanded and covered vast territories—an area which extended from the northwest of Yunnan province to the Kachin, Shan and Sky states in Myanmar. These writings, including folklore and other Tai chronicles that have been used in rewriting and revising interpretations, all speak of the "kingdom of the White Flower Mao Luang Kohsampee" or the "Mao Luang federation" which was a united and prosperous kingdom, having mighty armies able to extend its authority up to Kunming, Burma and the territories of Laos, Chiang Mai and Ayudhaya in later years. According to modern Tai Daikong interpretation, Tai Daikong culture flourished—before the Lanna, Sukhothai or Ayudhaya kingdoms—under a

8 Nanthasingha (1997).
9 Chao Hong Yuen and Sompong (1997).

famous Tai leader or hero: Chao Sua Khan Fa of Mao kingdom who unified the Tai race into a strong united people. However, this kingdom disintegrated in the sixteenth century due to massive attacks by the Chinese army.

Whether Chao Sua Khan Fa and other heroes mentioned in the chronicles really existed and the Mao kingdom was truly a large and powerful state may not be such important issues,[10] but the important thing is that the writings and interpretation of Tai chronicles in the past decade are the constitution of a significant or real history. It is an attempt to reconstruct a sense of Tai ethnic identity through the creation of an historical consciousness or ideals of the Tai race. Almost every line of the *Muang Tai Chronicles* depicts the yearnings for the glories of the Tai people of the fourteenth century. During the period of Chao Sua Khan Fa, the Tai were one country with one and the same king, united and inseparable, free of oppression by any other people's rule. The Tai chronicles also record accounts of many major battles between the Mao kingdom and the Ming dynasty of the Chinese Imperial Court in the fifteenth century to remind the Tai people to enshrine in their memory that at one time Muang Tai used to be independent and that their ancestors sacrificed their blood and lives to preserve that independence. Even though the Tai people were attacked by the Chinese and the Burmese, they tried to defend themselves and were able to revitalise their strength many times until finally they were broken up into small states under the rule of China and Burma, a situation which persists up to the present time.

The perplexing problem of shifting and changing ethnic boundaries among the Tai in Daikong in their relations with other ethnic groups in Yunnan, the reshaping of their own ethnicity with reference to their own sense of the past or the construction of Tai historical consciousness which began to emerge during the past decade may not involve only the yearning for past glories or the return to the security of the *chaopha* system, and may not be attempts to seek separation and independence from Chinese rule. On the contrary, we are witnessing the regaining of control over the production of knowledge or the power of self-definition. Amidst increasing tensions with other ethnic groups in Daikong, the Tai try to differentiate themselves by redefining their Tai-ness in the vocabulary of history, kinship and religious rituals; and, most of all, by resisting Chinese supremacy.

---

10 cf. Wyatt (1984:33–35).

The reconstruction of Tai ethnic identity takes place within the context of power relations with the Han Chinese. It is part of an attempt to seek self-determination which begins necessarily with the power of self-definition. In this light, the reinterpretation of *Muang Tai Chronicles* stresses that there was little disparity in terms of greatness between the Tai *chaopha* and the Chinese Emperor, and between the Tai kingdom and China of the past.

After the revolution of 1949, Daikong became a prefecture within the province of Yunnan. Although China officially referred to Daikong as an "autonomous prefecture" of the Tai and Jingpo, in reality the Tai were under the direct rule of China. Soon after the revolution, the *chaopha* were dethroned and the palaces dismantled and burnt to the ground. The *chaopha* and family members were incarcerated, beaten up, abused and put to death in the presence of the Tai populace. The ricefields that the Tai people cleared and cultivated and from which they earned their livelihood for hundreds of years were turned into state property, snatched from the control and management of the Tai people. Conflicts and upheavals which have characterised Chinese politics during the decades after the Communist revolution also resulted in economic crises for the Tai community. The abundance of food and bountiful crops were replaced by hunger and starvation under the collective farming system and commune plans.

After 1976, although Chinese official policies became more transparent and the Tai people began to enjoy more freedom of self-determination, the power relations between the Tai and the Han Chinese developed into a sort of confrontation between two interest groups, each group vying to expand its own freedom and curb the liberty of the other. In their relations of confrontation, the target of each side was not a conflict or a fight to the death with the other side; but rather to alter the positions in the power relations that benefit the opposite side and to fortify the positions that benefit one's own side and prevent one's own side from turning into something else.[11] From this perspective, Tai ethnic identity is situationally reconstructed as a weapon in the clash of social, economic and political interests in the relations between the Tai and the Chinese and other ethnic groups. Therefore self-definition is a matter of power relations expressed by symbolism[12] which the Chinese and the Tai, representing two interest groups

---

11 Foucault (1982:221).
12 Cohen (1974:xi).

(including other ethnic groups in Daikong territory), are contending and striving for in the process of allocation, preservation and utilisation of power.

Self-definition is therefore the creation of historical consciousness.[13] In the interest of building a political process of differentiation, many cultural symbols are utilised in order to arouse emotions and feelings and to prompt group members to resist dominance. Cultural symbols and ethic groupings are utilised in forming organisations and creating unification to oppose the other interest groups. The employment of ethnic symbols is an effective strategy, as ethnic symbols are able to resolve various problems of organisational arrangements, such as cultural emblems of ethnic groups that confirm common ancestry, and kinship and marriage traditions that ban outsiders from joining the group.

In this light, the reconstruction of Tai ethnic identity may take on many forms as the Tai adapt themselves to the changing needs and new social reality of modern times. Cultural symbols may be utilised as symbolic resistance against cultural domination within the power relations with the Han Chinese, age-old traditions could be modified to form a new organisation, and old cultural traditions can be reinterpreted to constitute a new set of social rules.

Symbolic Resistance and Reconstruction of Ethnic Identity

From fieldwork carried out in the Kachin Hills in northern Burma over 50 years ago, Edmund Leach[14] offered his view on the criteria for establishing the ethnic identity of the Tai people who settled in various locations in the Shan State of Burma and neighbouring territories. A first general criterion is that all Tai settlements are associated with wet-rice cultivation. Tai settlements mostly occur along the river valleys or in pockets of level country in the hills. Such settlements are always found associated with irrigated paddy land suitable for replanting rice seedlings and growing a variety of rice which is their staple diet. A second and most important criterion of group identity is that all Tai are Buddhists of the Theravada sect, devoutly observing their religious precepts and practices. The

---

13 Tapp (1989).
14 Leach (1954:30–31).

third criterion of Tai group identity is that all Tai settlements are members of a Tai-type petty state. These three criteria are closely intertwined. The prosperity and surplus production that come from plains of wet paddy imply membership of a Tai petty state which implies Buddhism.

Even though more than half a century has passed, the general criteria that Leach has observed still prevail as important criteria of how to conceptualise the category Shan or Tai. From this point of view, we will examine the reconstruction of ethnic identity and symbolic resistance of the Tai in Daikong on the basis of the three criteria mentioned above. Examples will be drawn from three cultural symbols of the Tai, namely: rice as the symbol of the Tai peasant community, *poi* festivals as the symbol of belief and devotion in Buddhism and the invention of marriage rules and traditions as part of the community reproduction process in Daikong.

Rice: Symbolic Resistance against Cultural Supremacy

Rice has played an important role in the way of life and social development of the Tai Daikong and other Tai groups since time immemorial. Tai society everywhere developed from a small rice-producing peasant community, with customs and traditions emanating from dialectical relationships between rice and man within the ecological niche of the river valley. Rice is not only a plant that suits the Daikong ecological system but also the staple food of the Tai; rice economy lays the foundation of social organisation and production technology as well as the belief system and world view of the Tai. For this reason, it is not surprising to find that almost all Tai communities are peasant communities, practising wet-rice cultivation; labour-exchange groups and land and irrigation committees are among the most important social and resource management organisations; households are the basic unit of production and consumption; and kinsmen are important bases for creating political and social alliances.

The Tai have a saying that mentions the old domicile of their ancestors over a thousand years ago: "wherever the water is clear and the grass is tender, the Tai people will build houses, clear forest land for ricefields and make a living". Rice cultivation as a way of life has been an important basis for expansion of the original Tai colonisation of the river valleys associated with the maintenance of trade routes extending from Yunnan to India.[15] The peasant communities have been able to support themselves economically without very intricate production systems other than to clear the forest into ricefields. When new peasant communities began to grow in numbers, such new communities attracted and accumulated greater strength and more surplus produce, thus expanding themselves into larger communities which would develop in time into Tai-type petty states.

For centuries of Sino-Tai historical relations, "rice" has played a crucial role in the practice of political supremacy. From many historical records,[16] it was mentioned that after the Tai lost the last battle against the Chinese armies in the fifteenth century, the Chinese succeeded in taking the Mao kingdom. It is apparent that, from then on, Tai glory had departed. In place of a solid kingdom, we have now semi-independent principalities. In the sixteenth century, Tai principalities east of the Irrawaddy River became the Shan states and were never free from Burmese rule, though from time to time various states gained a nominal independence. The Tai principalities to the east and northeast of Muang Mao were annexed to China and remained part of Yunnan province till today. The *chaopha* of each principality was appointed directly by the Chinese Imperial Court to rule over his own territory independently and was answerable directly only to the Imperial Court. As the Tai Daikong now *remember* it, Tai rice, especially from Muang Chae Fang, was of superb quality, relished by the Chinese Emperor and ministers of the Imperial Court. In the historical consciousness of the Tai, rice becomes a symbol of political superiority and domination.

Moreover, during the three decades following the Communist revolution, the Tai people had to suffer unprecedented shortage of rice for consumption as a result of production problems arising from collective farming and the commune systems, including the fact that rice production from Daikong was heavily siphoned off to feed labour forces in other parts of China.

During the past two decades following administrative reforms under the leadership of Deng Xiaoping, the Chinese government abolished the collective

15 Leach (1954:38–39).
16 See, for example, Elias (1876); Parker (1892); Scott and Hardiman (1900–01); Cochrane (1910); Chea (1995).

farming and commune systems, opening the way for farmers to have a free hand in production and sale of their produce. Throughout this period, the Tai peasants took advantage of this favourable situation to concentrate on production and trade to quickly raise their status. The demand for agricultural products increased rapidly, thus making prices advance accordingly. The fertility of farmland in Daikong enabled the Tai peasants to produce cash crops all year round. The Tai peasants turned into expert traders and producers of cash crops. They have developed an ability to predict market demand and they have the skills to bargain for better prices for commercial crops with Chinese merchants on equal terms.

In Daikong prefecture, rice production is carried out during the months of April to October. Thereafter, the Tai peasants normally divide their farmland for growing a variety of commercial crops such as wheat, watermelons and peas. All these products will be sold to the Chinese traders who come to buy them directly from the fields. In addition, the peasant households grow a variety of vegetables for family consumption as well as for sale in Muang Khon open market to earn cash income all year round.

Non-glutinous rice is the produce that brings in good income for the Tai people every year. Income from rice sales accounts for nearly half of the total earnings that a household obtains from the sale of agricultural produce each year. The price of rice fluctuates according to the volume and each year's market demand. During the months of June and July, rice supply becomes short in many parts of China, pushing up the price, and rice merchants come by the Tai village almost every week to buy rice. However, the Tai villagers who definitely have surplus stock—because they never use or consume up to half of the quantity they produce in each year—prefer not to sell rice at this time of the year and, instead, prefer to sell the rice during the months of October to November when rice stocks begin to flow into the market and prices begin to fall. The Tai people stock up their silos with new rice and sell the previous year's rice to the Chinese traders.

If the Tai sold rice during the month of August, they would make 25 to 30 per cent more money from the sales. When we asked why such shrewd traders do not choose to maximise the profit from the rice sales as with other products, the answer we invariably obtained was that the villagers want to hold on to the rice stock in order to have the feeling of security in life.

One night, at the wedding party of Sam Fong's nephew, we found what may be the real reason behind this odd behaviour when an elder of Lak Chang retold this story.

> Our forefathers had to deliver the best rice to the Chinese Court for many generations… But nowadays, the Tai descendants sell *left-over* rice they don't want to eat to the *khay* people. It makes me feel good.

The words of this elder made a large group of Tai peasants who were drinking at the party burst into thunderous laughter as if these words had touched a tender spot in their hearts and provoked common feelings among the circle of listeners.

In reality, we probably would not be able to arrive at an understanding of the rice-selling conduct on purely economic grounds since this behaviour is guided by another set of values. To fully grasp the meaning of it, one has to begin with an understanding of "rice" as a symbol of resistance against political dominance, which may help to explain the situation the Tai are currently facing, both in terms of their adaptation to the market mechanism and as a means of expressing their resistance to a more powerful ethnic majority.

By viewing rice as a cultural symbol in Tai society, we can clearly see that the Tai have changed rice from the symbol of a subjugated community to that of a respectable one, from being a subordinate to that of a challenger, altering the inferior position of relationship to one of equal terms by the process of historical retrospection. The use of rice as a symbol of Tai community has given special meaning to the awareness of being subjected to economic and political dominance. The sale of rice that is left over after consumption to the Han Chinese is one form of symbolic resistance. Rice becomes the symbol that gives meaning to the experience the Tai are currently facing, both in terms of self-adjustment to capitalism that came with the Chinese and as symbolic opposition to political dominance, while at the same time it is also a tool for presenting the Tai ethnic identity.

Poi Festivals, Buddhism and Tai Community

Apart from rice being used as a symbol of resistance, the holding of Buddhist religious events—especially *poi para* or *poi prachao*—is another form of expression whereby cultural traditions are reinterpreted in the formation of new social organisations uniting fellow Tai in competing with other ethnic groups.

Throughout history, Buddhism has played a fundamental role in the shaping of Tai ethnic identity. The nucleus of being Tai today is the belief in Buddhism. The Tai differentiate themselves from neighbouring ethnic groups by citing one main reason: the others are not Buddhists. By this reasoning, being Tai means professing the Buddhist faith; other people who do not believe in the Buddhist religion of the Theravada sect are looked upon as outsiders and are segregated outside the Tai ethnic boundaries. Buddhism is paramount at the cultural level and also exerts a great deal of influence on village social life. The significance of Buddhism in the life of the Tai can be measured by the time, resources and labour that ordinary Tai villagers devote to Buddhist religious affairs, especially in arranging *poi* or merit-making festivities.

In the past, *poi* festivals were affairs in which rich households in the village dedicated themselves as sponsors for the purchase of Buddhist statues, Tripitaka cabinets as well as various items for presentation to the temple, including celebration feasts to which all villagers were invited to join. *Poi* festivals were good occasions to celebrate life after harvest, to reaffirm positive ties with friends, relatives, neighbours and all members of the village invited by the sponsors to join the celebrations. *Poi* festivals were also significant occasions for merit making and creating self-esteem for the sponsors, as well as playing an important part in socialising the new generations of young men and women with duties and training regarding their roles and responsibilities toward the community. The group of young men had an important role acting as representatives of the sponsors in travelling to purchase Buddhist statues as well as other items for presentation to the temple. These young men were also the main labour force repairing the temple prior to the *poi* festival. The maiden group, on the other hand, had the main task of decorating and beautifying the temple and helping the sponsors arranging flowers and cooking food for the feasts.

At present, however, *poi* festivals sponsored by various households in the village have become scarce because increasing intensification of agricultural production has saddled villagers with increased work on their farms and trading all year round. The Tai villagers now prefer to organise *poi* festivals at temples where every household in the village becomes a joint sponsor, with the village elders acting as organising committee. *Poi para* festivals are similar in nature to *poi* festivals in olden days in all respects with the exception that funding for the festivals is derived entirely from donations by every household and the feasts are held on the temple grounds. *Poi para* or *poi chong* festivals have become an important occasion for joint participation by every household in the village in cleaning and making the temple beautiful as well as preparing food and wine for the feast.

During the past decade, *poi chong* festivals have become important functions that various villages organise on a grand scale by inviting guests from outside the village to join the festivities. These festivals have begun to take the shape of competition between villages in the vicinity to see which village can outdo the others. If in the previous year, Lak Chang village was able to arrange a *poi* festival on a grand scale and became the talk of people in that area, then in the following year another Tai village would try to organise a *poi* festival that was even grander and more lavishly entertaining in order to make Lak Chang and other villages lose face. In so doing, Tai villages have to try to arrange grander and grander festivals year after year. Consequently, *poi* festivals have undergone a transformation from being activities that concentrated upon competition and display of wealth and prestige between various households of the same village to instead becoming competitions between villages.

This new form of *poi* festival places a great deal of emphasis on the unity and cohesion among villagers and at the same time strengthens ethnic identity through the display of religious symbols. *Poi* festivals have become rituals which stress religious devotion to the Buddhism of the Tai people. Through these rituals, the stage is set whereby the Tai are set apart from other ethnic groups. At the same time, displays of affluence and social prestige at the village level are now expressed through other forms of social display such as organising funerals or wedding parties on a grand scale to give impressions of esteem and honour at individual or household levels.

Marriage, Farmland and the Reproduction of an Imagined Community

Nowadays, every Tai in Daikong is a citizen of the People's Republic of China. Holding Chinese citizenship, however, does not imply assimilation into the Han ethnic group. On the contrary, it is a part of an adjustment to a social situation where a number of ethnic groups coexist together, and each group speaks a number of different languages and dialects. To a certain extent, the Tai have adapted themselves by learning to speak, read and write the Chinese language, eating with chopsticks and building Chinese-style houses, all of which are part of their adaptation to present-day social conditions. The Tai emulations of Chinese characteristics are not just distorted imitations but become, rather, constitutive elements in Tai lives. The ethnic identity of the Tai Daikong is constructed in a continual process, not only by external forces and labelling by outsiders with whom they interact, but also by their own socio-cultural process of creating a self-definition. In certain situations, the acceptance of Han characteristics is real. Conversely, in other situations, the stress on ethnic difference and group identity may be more advantageous, especially in terms of using ethnic boundaries and markers to exclude and deny other groups the access to scarce resources, particularly farmland.

In Daikong, the best farmlands belong to Tai villagers whose ancestors were pioneer settlers in the central plain of Muang Khon many centuries ago. Each Tai village maintains the distinct characteristics of an autonomous unit, not only in terms of physical appearances but also in historical background and socio-economic formations which are clearly distinguishable from other villages. Fellow villagers have a strong sense of belonging to the same social unit, yet they live separately from Tai people of other villages in the vicinity.

During the past two decades, farmland has become increasingly valued due to expanded markets and increased demands for agricultural products. Increasing demands from the market have resulted in more intensification of land-use and increasing ethnic tensions over landholdings, as the Han Chinese migrants began moving in and laying claim to a share of the village's paddy fields. The Tai peasants tried to refute the claim, citing the reason that the *khay* were not real members of the village because their forefathers had no part in the pioneer work of clearing the forestland in this area. The *khay* therefore had no right to the use of farmland unlike the Tai offspring of Lak Chang village who have a right as direct descendants.

In this case, the reproduction and reconfirmation of Tai ethnic identity are attempts to proclaim legitimate rights over land inheritance and, at the same time, to exclude outsiders from access to resources that are scarce and essential to the local economy. The reconstruction of ethnic identity thus plays a crucial role in the struggle over scarce resources. However, the struggle between the Tai and the Chinese is not merely a struggle over land and property rights, it is also a struggle over the appropriation of symbols, a struggle over how the past and present shall be understood, a struggle to identify causes and assess blame, a struggle which has become a contentious effort to give meaning to local history and ethnic identity. In this struggle, the Tai peasants have modified their cultural traditions in various ways. For example, marriage practices have been reshaped so that endogamous marriage is now the rule, traditional practices of respect toward the elders have been revived and the council of elders now plays an important role in supervising various affairs of the village.

Symbolic resistance against cultural domination as expressed in the selling of leftover rice, the endogamous marriage rule, the organisation of *poi* festivals, the reaffirmation of ethnic identity to legitimise land rights, the construction of historical consciousness by reinterpreting ancient chronicles, the relearning of Tai languages in villages and the Tai Association in Muang Khon, all attest to the role of the Tai people in actively constructing, perpetuating and transforming cultural values and traditions in the interest of building political processes of differentiation and commonality. Amidst increasing conflicts and competition with the Han Chinese over scarce resources, the Tai try to differentiate themselves from the *khay* by redefining their Tai-ness in the vocabulary of history, kinship, marriage, land rights and religious rituals. We are thus witnessing the invention of their real history, the production of ethnic consciousness in creating a unified political identity and an imagined Tai community.

However, Tai ethnic identity is not a ready-made entity, fixed and permanent, but a conscious choice of identifications and affiliations that are picked up because they seemed advantageous under present conditions. The Tai choose to invent new traditions—such as endogamous marriage—and they choose to modify old ones—for instance the *poi* festivals—in order to construct new principles of social organisations which emphasise social unity in the context of increased competition with other ethnic groups. The construction and reconstruction of Tai ethnic identity thus take place within the context of an adaptation aimed at meeting the changing needs of modern times. The case of the Tai Daikong underlines the fluidity of tradition as a weapon which the weak can use to fight for and protect their interests.

The Tai construct, reconstruct and modify value systems to conform with changing socio-economic and political contexts. Ethnic differentiation from other groups thus becomes an important issue of power relations arising from a certain set of conditions such as competition for scarce resources and the clash of interests. In such power relations, the Tai people find themselves in a more advantageous position by redefining their ethnic boundaries and their Tai-ness through the invention of their real history and modifications of various cultural symbols.

Tai ethnic identity is thus a realm where culture and power are closely intertwined. An important point to be considered in defining what constitutes a Tai ethnic group concerns the nature of its subjective construction. This is deeply rooted in the image of themselves held by individuals, communities and polities, with each of these distinguished from others by particular historical, social and political contexts. The ethnic identity of the Tai Daikong is thus constructed in a continual process, not only by external forces and labelling by the Chinese and other outsiders with whom they interact, but also through their own socio-cultural process of creating a self-definition. The perplexing notion of the ethnic group is largely attributable to this imagined construction. Thus the Tai ethnic category can be examined only when we can account for the continual processes of imagined construction, both subjective and externally enforced, viewing them both together in their historical context. The Tai ethnic category is thus a complex and dynamic construct which takes place within the context of changing power relations and socio-economic conditions where the past is reconstructed to give meaning to the present and hope for the future.

BIBLIOGRAPHY

Akin Rabibhadana

1969 *The Organization of Thai Society in the Early Bangkok Period, 1782–1873.* Ithaca, New York: Cornell University Southeast Asia Program, Data Paper No. 74.

Anan Ganjanapan

1984 The partial commercialization of rice production in northern Thailand, 1890–1981. PhD thesis, Cornell University.

1994 Sathanapap Karn Wijai Pattanakarn Tang Sangkhom Lae Wattanatham Tai Yai (The state of knowledge on Tai Yai society and cultural development) in *Karn Suksa Wattanatham Chon Chart Tai* (Tai Cultural Studies). Bangkok: Office of the National Cultural Commission.

Anderson, Benedict R. O'G.

1983 *Imagined Communities: reflections on the origin and spread of nationalism.* London: Verso.

Anuman Rajadhon, Phya

1961 *Life and Ritual in Old Siam.* New Haven: HRAF Press.

Banchop Panthummeka

1983 *Ka Le Maan Tai Nai Rat Shan* (A journey with the Tai in Shan State). Bangkok: National Identity Commission, Office of the Prime Minister.

Bandit Paorangkha (trans.)

1994 Tamnan Muang Mok Khao Mao Luang (Legends of Muang Mao). Unpublished manuscript.

Bernstein, Thomas P.

1977 *Up to the Mountains and down to the Villages: the transfer of youth from urban to rural China.* New Haven: Yale University Press.

Burling, Robbins

1992　*Hill Farms and Paddy Fields: life in mainland Southeast Asia.* Arizona State University, Program for Southeast Asian Studies (Reprint edition).

Changli, Zhu

1990　A research on Pong—an ancient Shan state. *Proceedings of the 4th International Conference on Thai Studies,* Vol. 1, Kunming, China: Institute of Southeast Asian Studies.

Chao Hong Yuen and Sompong Wittayasakpan (trans.)

1997　Pongsawadarn Muang Tai (Muang Tai Chronicles) Tai Culture and History Project, unpublished manuscript.

Chao Tzang Yawnghwe

1987　*The Shan of Burma.* Singapore: Institute of Southeast Asian Studies.

Chattip Nartsupha

1984　*Baan and Muang.* Bangkok: Sang Sarn.

1991　*Wattanatham Thai Kap Krabuankarn Plien Plang Sangkhom* (Thai culture and social change movements). Bangkok: Chulalongkorn University Press.

Chattip Nartsupha and Renoo Wichasilpa

1995　State of knowledge on Tai Ahom history. In *Karn Suksa Wattanatham Chonchart Tai* (Tai Cultural Studies). Bangkok: National Cultural Office.

Chayan Vaddhanaphuti

1984　Cultural and ideological reproduction in rural northern Thai Society. PhD thesis, Stanford University.

Chea Yanchong

1988　The ancient culture of the Tai people. *Journal of the Siam Society* 76: 227–244.

1990　More thoughts on the ancient culture of the Tai people: the impact of the Hua Xia culture on it, and its implications, in *Proceedings of the 4th International Conference on Thai Studies,* Kunming (11–13 May), Vol. 4, pp. 180–201.

1995　Tai Lue Sipsong Panna before the revolution. In *Sipsong Panna.* Bangkok: National Cultural Office.

Cochrane, Wilbur W.
1910   The Northern Shan: a brief historical account. In Leslie Milne, *Shans at home*. London: John Murray.
1915   *The Shans*. Vol. 1. Rangoon: Government Printing Press.

Coedes, George
1968   *The Indianized States of Southeast Asia*. Honolulu: East West Center Press.

Cohen, Abner
1974   *Two-dimensional Man: an essay on the anthropology of power and symbolism in complex society*. London: Routledge and Kegan Paul.

Collis, Maurice S.
1938   *Lord of the Sun Set: a tour of the Shan States*. London: Faber and Faber.

Comeroff, Jean and John Comeroff
1991   *Of Revelation and Revolution: christianity and consciousness in South Africa*. Chicago: University of Chicago Press.

Condominas, George
1990   *From Lawa to Mon, from Saa' to Thai: historical and anthropological aspects of Southeast Asian social space*. Canberra: Australian National University.

Davis, Richard
1984   *Muang Metaphysics: a study of northern Thai myth and ritual*. Bangkok: Pandora.

DeVos, G. and Romanucci-Ross, L.
1975   *Ethnic Identity*. Palo Alto: Mayfield Publications.

DeVos. G. ed.
1976   *Responses to Change: society, culture and personality*. New York: D. Van Nostrand.

Dodd, William C.
1923   *The Tai Race: elder brother of the Chinese*. Cedar Rapids, Ia.: Torch Press.

Drucker, P.
1967   The Potlatch. In G. Dalton, ed. *Tribal and Peasant Economies*. New York: Natural History Press.

Durrenberger, Paul E.

1983   The Shan rocket festival: Buddhist and non-Buddhist aspects of Shan religion. *Journal of the Siam Society* 71:63–74.

Durrenberger, Paul E. and Nicola Tannenbaum

1990   *Analytical Perspectives on Shan Agriculture and Village Economy.* New Haven: Yale University Southeast Asian Studies.

Eberhard, Wolfram

1968   *The Local Cultures of South and East China.* Alide Eberhard (trans.) Leiden: E.J. Brill.

Eberhardt, Nancy Jean

1988a Knowledge, belief, and reasoning: moral development and culture acquisition in a Shan village of Northwest Thailand. PhD thesis, University of Illinois.

1988b Siren song: negotiating gender images in rural Shan village, in Nancy Jean Eberhardt (ed.), *Gender, Power and the Construction of the Moral Order: studies from the Thai periphery.* Madison: University of Wisconsin-Madison, Center for Southeast Asian Studies, Monograph No. 4.

Elias, Ney

1876   *Introductory Sketch of the History of the Shans in Upper Burma and West Yunnan.* Calcutta: Foreign Department Service.

Foucault, Michel

1982   Afterword: the subject and power. In Hubert L. Dreyfus and Paul Rabinow (eds), *Michel Foucault: beyond structuralism and hermaneutics.* Chicago: University of Chicago Press.

Friedman, Jonathan

1994   *Cultural Identity, Global Process.* London: Sage.

Garthew, M.

1952   The history of the Thai in Yunnan, 2205 BC–1253 AD. *Journal of the Siam Society* 40(1):1–38.

Gates, Henry L. Jr, ed.

1986   *"Race", Writing and Difference.* Chicago: University of Chicago Press.

Geertz, Clifford
1973   *The Interpretations of Culture.* New York: Basic Books.

Geertz, Hildred
1961   *The Javanese Family.* Glencoe: The Free Press.

Griggs, William C.
1902   *Shan Folk Lore Stories.* Philadelphia: n.p.

Hallet, Holt S.
1890   *A Thousand Miles on an Elephant in the Shan States.* Edinburgh and
        London: William Blackwood, Repr. 1988, Bangkok: White Lotus.

Harvey, G.E. and Barton, G.E.
1930   *Meng Mao Succession.* Burma Secretariat File, Imprint No. 99. HPD
        29/10/30, Rangoon.

Hillier, W.R.
1892   Notes on the manners, customs, religion, and superstitution of the tribes
        inhabiting the Shan States. *Indian Antiquary* 21: 116–121.

Hinton, William
1966   *Fanshen: a documentary of revolution in a Chinese village.* New York:
        Vintage.
1983   *Shen Fan: the continuing revolution in a Chinese village.* London: Secker
        and Warburg.

Hobsbawm, E. and T. Ranger, eds
1983   *The Invention of Tradition.* Cambridge: Cambridge University Press.

Hsieh Shih-Chung
1989   Ethnic-political adaptation and ethnic change of the Sipsong Panna Tai:
        an ethnohistorical analysis. PhD thesis, University of Washington.

Hsu, Francis L.K.
1963   *Clan, Caste and Club.* New York: Van Nostrand.

Iwata, Keiji and Michio Matsuoka
1967   Agricultural practices among Thai Yai, Thai Lu and certain hill tribes in
        Northern Thailand. *Nature and Life in Southeast Asia* 5: 295–312.

Izikowitz, Karl Gustav
1962   Notes about the Tai. *Bulletin of the Museum of Far Eastern Antiquities* 34: 73–91.

Kajorn Sukapanich
1982   *Kho Mun Prawatsart Samai Kon Tang Sukothai* (Historical Data of Pre-Sukothai Period). Bangkok: Kuru Sapha.

Kapadia, K.M.
1966   *Marriage and Family in India.* London: Oxford University Press.

Kelliher, Daniel
1992   *Peasant Power in China: the era of rural reform 1979–1989.* New Haven: Yale University Press.

Leach, Edmund R.
1954   *Political Systems of Highland Burma.* London: The Ashlore Press.

Lebar, Frank M., Gerald Hickey and John K. Musgrave
1964   *Ethnic Groups of Mainland Southeast Asia.* New Haven: HRAF Press.

Lehman, F.K.
1963   *The Structure of Chin Society.* Urbana: University of Illinois Press.

Lieberthal, Kenneth
1995   *Governing China: from revolution through reform.* New York: W.W. Norton.

Lilley, Rozanna
1990   Afterword: "ethnicity" and anthropology. In Gehan Wijeyewardene, ed. *Ethnic Groups across National Boundaries in Mainland Southeast Asia.* Singapore: Institute of Southeast Asian Studies.

Mandelbaum, David
1970   *Society in India.* Berkeley: University of California Press.

Meisner, Maurice
1977   *Mao's China.* New York: Free Press.

Milne, Leslie
1910   *Shans at Home.* London: John Murray.

Nanthasingha
1997 Prawatsart Tai Yai (Tai Yai history) Thai Culture and History Studies
      Project. Unpublished manuscript.

Nithi Oewsriwongse
1990 Khon Tai Ma Chak Non Duai Lae Khon Tai Yoo Tii Nii Duai (Tai
      people came from their and Thai people also lived here) *Silpa
      Wattanatham* 11(12): 76–82.

Parker, E.H.
1893 The old Thai or Shan empire of Western Yunnan. *China Review* 20:
      338–346.

Patai, Raphael
1971 *Society, Culture and Change in the Middle East.* Philadelphia: University
      of Pennsylvania Press.

Pattaya Saihoo
1959 The Shan of Burma: An Ethnographic Survey. BLitt thesis, Oxford
      University.

Pe Maung Tin
1961 Women in the Inscriptions in Pagan. *50th Anniversary Publication,*
      Burma Research Society.

Potter, Shulamith
1976 *Family Life in a Northern Thai Village.* Berkeley: University of California
      Press.

Reynard, Ron
1988 Social change in the Shan States under the British, 1886–1942. In Prakai
      Nontawase (ed.), *Changes in Northern Thailand and the Shan States,
      1886–1940.* Singapore: Institute of Southeast Asian Studies.

Rujaya Arpakorn, M.R.
1994 Sathannapap Kong Ong Kwam Roo Kiew Kap Pattanakarn Tang
      Sangkhom Lae Wattanatham Kong Klum Tai Lue Nai Pajjuban
      (The state of knowledge of Tai Lue social and cultural development).
      In *Sipsong Panna.* Bangkok: Office of the National Cultural Commission.

Sahlins, Marshall

1985   *Islands of History.* Chicago: University of Chicago Press.

Said, Edward W.

1978   *Orientalism.* New York: Pantheon Books.

Saimong Mangrai, Sao

1963   *The Shan States and the British Annexation.* Ithaca, New York: Cornell University, Southeast Asia Program, Data Paper No. 57.

Sargent, Inge

1994   *Twilight over Burma: my life as a Shan princess.* Honolulu: University of Hawaii Press.

Saskia, S. Yasmin

1996   Twentieth century biographies of a community: brokering the Tai-Ahom. A paper presented at the *6th International Conference on Thai Studies,* Chiang Mai, Thailand.

Scott, James George

1936   *Scott of the Shan Hills: orders and impressions.* London: Murray.

Scott, James George and John Percy Hardiman

1900   *Gazetteer of Upper Burma and the Shan States,* Pt. 1, Vol. 1. Rangoon: Superintendent of Government Printing and Stationery.

Shalardchai Ramitanondha

1986   *Pii Chao Nai* (Spirits of the Lords). Chiang Mai: Text Book Project, Chiang Mai University.

Sompong Wittayasakphan

1999   *Prawatsart Sangkhom Lae Watthanatham Tai Yai* (Social and Cultural History of Tai Yai). Research Monograph, Social and Cultural History of the Tai People Project, Thailand Research Fund.

Spiro, Melford E.

1977   *Kinship and Marriage in Burma: cultural and psychodynamic analysis.* Berkeley: University of California Press.

1982   *Buddhism and Society: a great tradition and its Burmese vicissitudes.* Second edition. Berkeley: University of California Press.

Srisak Wullipodom and Suchit Wongthes

1991   *Tai Lue, Tai Yai Lae Thai Siam* (Tai Lue, Tai Yai and Siamese Thai).
Bangkok: Silpa Wattanatham.

Sumitr Pitiphat

1980   The religion and beliefs of the black Tai, and a note on the study of
cultural origins. *Journal of the Siam Society* 68(1): 29–38.

Sunetra Chutintaranondha

1991   Thin Kumnert Chon Chart Tai: Kwam Tang Kong Ranab Tang Kwam
Kid (The origin of the Tai nation: the diverse views). *Silpa Wattanatham*
12(5): 142–155

Tan, Leshan

1993   Power and prestige in a Chinese Shan village. A paper presented at the
5th International Conference on Thai Studies, SOAS, London.

Tanabe, Shigeharu

1991   *Religious Traditions among Tai Ethnic Groups: a selected bibliography.*
Ayutthaya: Ayutthaya Historical Study Centre.

Tannenbaum, Nicola

1982   Agricultural decision making among the Shan of Maehongson province,
Northwest Thailand. PhD thesis, University of Iowa.

1989   Power and its Shan transformation. In S. Russell (ed.), *Ritual, Power, and
Economy in Mainland Southeast Asia.* Dekalb: Northern Illinois
University, Center for Southeast Asian Studies, Occasional Paper No. 14.

Tapp, Nicholas

1989   *Sovereignty and Rebellion: the white Hmong of Northern Thailand.*
Singapore: Oxford University Press.

Tawee Sawangpanyakul

1986   *Tamnan Puenmuang Sipsong Panna* (Sipsong Panna local folktales).
Chiang Mai: Chiang Mai Book Center.

Taylor, Robert

1988   British policy and the Shan States, 1886–1942. In Prakai Nontawase
(ed.), *Changes in Northern Thailand and the Shan States, 1886–1940.*
Singapore: Institute of Southeast Asian Studies.

Terwiel, B.J., Anthony Diller and Choltira Sattayawattana
1990   *Khon Tai* (*Derm*) *Mai Dai Yoo Tii Nii* (Tai People did not live here).
        Bangkok: Muang Boran Publication.

Terwiel, Baas J.
1979   Tai funeral customs: towards a reconstruction of archaic-Tai ceremonies.
        Anthropos 74: 393–432.

Thorp, E.
1945   *Quite Skies on the Salween.* London: John Murray.

T'ien Ju-K'ang
1986   *Religious Cults of the Pai-I along the Burma–Yunnan Border.*
        Ithaca, New York: Cornell University, Southeast Asia Program.

Tongtam Nartchamnong
1991   Karn Khon Khwa Kam Wa Tai (Researches on the word Tai). *Silpa
        Wattanatham* 12(5):136–145

Vogel, Ezra
1969   *Canton under Communism.* New York: Harper.

Wendt, A.
1987   Novelists, historians and the art of remembering. In Hooper, A., et al.,
        Class and Culture in the Pacific. Suva and Auckland: Institute of Pacific
        Studies of the University of the South Pacific and Centre for Pacific
        Studies of the University of Auckland.

Wijeyawardene, Gehan
1993   Ethnicity and nation: the Tai in Burma, Thailand and China
        (Sipsongpanna and Dehong). A paper presented at the *5th International
        Conference on Thai Studies*, SOAS, London.

Wijeyewardene, Gehan, ed.
1990   *Ethnic Groups across National Boundaries in Mainland Southeast Asia.*
        Singapore: Institute of Southeast Asian Studies.

Woodthorpe, R.G.
1896   The country of the Shans. *Geographical Journal* 7:577–602.

World Bank
1993   *World Tables 1993*. Baltimore: Johns Hopkins University Press.

Wyatt, David K.
1984   *Thailand: a short history*. Bangkok: Thai Watana Panich.

Yawnghwe, Chao Tzang
1987   *The Shan of Burma: memoirs of a Shan in exile*. Singapore: Institute of Southeast Asian Studies.

Yos Santasombat
1992   *Mae Ying Si Kai Tua* (Community and commoditisation of sexuality in Thai society). Bangkok: Local Development Institute.
1996   *Tha Kwien: a preliminary analysis on the adaptation of Thai peasant community amidst the enclosure of industrial culture*. Bangkok: Kob Fai.

Yule, H.
1858   *A Mission to the Court of Ava in 1855*. London: Richardson and McCleod.

Zhao Hongyun and Ke Yuanxiuo
1990   On the relationships between Dehong Dai and Ahom Dai. In *Proceedings of the 4th International Conference on Thai Studies*, Kunming, Vol. 3: 402–405.

Zhu, Liangwen
1992   *The Dai or the Tai and their Architecture and Customs in South China*. Bangkok: DD Books.

INDEX